CSU MONTEREY BAY LIBRARY

3 0001 00149518 5

P9-AGU-936

RATTLING CHAINS

TRANSGRESSIONS: CULTURAL STUDIES AND EDUCATION

Volume 89

Series Editor:
Shirley R. Steinberg, *University of Calgary, Canada*

Founding Editor:
Joe L. Kincheloe (1950-2008) *The Paulo and Nita Freire International Project for Critical Pedagogy*

Editorial Board

Jon Austin, *University of Southern Queensland, Australia*
Norman Denzin, *University of Illinois, Champaign-Urbana, USA*
Rhonda Hammer, *University of California Los Angeles, USA*
Nikos Metallinos, *Concordia University, Canada*
Christine Quail, *McMaster University, Canada*
Ki Wan Sung, *Kyung Hee University, Seoul, Korea*

This book series is dedicated to the radical love and actions of Paulo Freire, Jesus "Pato" Gomez, and Joe L. Kincheloe.

Cultural studies provides an analytical toolbox for both making sense of educational practice and extending the insights of educational professionals into their labors. In this context *Transgressions: Cultural Studies and Education* provides a collection of books in the domain that specify this assertion. Crafted for an audience of teachers, teacher educators, scholars and students of cultural studies and others interested in cultural studies and pedagogy, the series documents both the possibilities of and the controversies surrounding the intersection of cultural studies and education. The editors and the authors of this series do not assume that the interaction of cultural studies and education devalues other types of knowledge and analytical forms. Rather the intersection of these knowledge disciplines offers a rejuvenating, optimistic, and positive perspective on education and educational institutions. Some might describe its contribution as democratic, emancipatory, and transformative. The editors and authors maintain that cultural studies helps free educators from sterile, monolithic analyses that have for too long undermined efforts to think of educational practices by providing other words, new languages, and fresh metaphors. Operating in an interdisciplinary cosmos, *Transgressions: Cultural Studies and Education* is dedicated to exploring the ways cultural studies enhances the study and practice of education. With this in mind the series focuses in a non-exclusive way on popular culture as well as other dimensions of cultural studies including social theory, social justice and positionality, cultural dimensions of technological innovation, new media and media literacy, new forms of oppression emerging in an electronic hyperreality, and postcolonial global concerns. With these concerns in mind cultural studies scholars often argue that the realm of popular culture is the most powerful educational force in contemporary culture. Indeed, in the twenty-first century this pedagogical dynamic is sweeping through the entire world. Educators, they believe, must understand these emerging realities in order to gain an important voice in the pedagogical conversation.

Without an understanding of cultural pedagogy's (education that takes place outside of formal schooling) role in the shaping of individual identity – youth identity in particular –

the role educators play in the lives of their students will continue to fade. Why do so many of our students feel that life is incomprehensible and devoid of meaning? What does it mean, teachers wonder, when young people are unable to describe their moods, their affective affiliation to the society around them. Meanings provided young people by mainstream institutions often do little to help them deal with their affective complexity, their difficulty negotiating the rift between meaning and affect. School knowledge and educational expectations seem as anachronistic as a ditto machine, not that learning ways of rational thought and making sense of the world are unimportant.

But school knowledge and educational expectations often have little to offer students about making sense of the way they feel, the way their affective lives are shaped. In no way do we argue that analysis of the production of youth in an electronic mediated world demands some "touchy-feely" educational superficiality. What is needed in this context is a rigorous analysis of the interrelationship between pedagogy, popular culture, meaning making, and youth subjectivity. In an era marked by youth depression, violence, and suicide such insights become extremely important, even life saving. Pessimism about the future is the common sense of many contemporary youth with its concomitant feeling that no one can make a difference.

If affective production can be shaped to reflect these perspectives, then it can be reshaped to lay the groundwork for optimism, passionate commitment, and transformative educational and political activity. In these ways cultural studies adds a dimension to the work of education unfilled by any other sub-discipline. This is what Transgressions: Cultural Studies and Education seeks to produce – literature on these issues that makes a difference. It seeks to publish studies that help those who work with young people, those individuals involved in the disciplines that study children and youth, and young people themselves improve their lives in these bizarre times.

Rattling Chains

Exploring Social Justice in Education

Edited by

Louis G. Denti
California State University, USA

and

Patricia A. Whang
California State University, USA

SENSE PUBLISHERS
ROTTERDAM / BOSTON / TAIPEI

A C.I.P. record for this book is available from the Library of Congress.

ISBN 978-94-6209-105-4 (paperback)
ISBN 978-94-6209-106-1 (hardback)
ISBN 978-94-6209-107-8 (e-book)

Published by: Sense Publishers,
P.O. Box 21858, 3001 AW Rotterdam, The Netherlands
https://www.sensepublishers.com

Printed on acid-free paper

All rights reserved © 2012 Sense Publishers

No part of this work may be reproduced, stored in a retrieval system, or transmitted in any form or
by any means, electronic, mechanical, photocopying, microfilming, recording or otherwise, without
written permission from the Publisher, with the exception of any material supplied specifically for the
purpose of being entered and executed on a computer system, for exclusive use by the purchaser of
the work.

TABLE OF CONTENTS

ACKNOWLEDGEMENTS

My (Lou) sincere and heartfelt appreciation to all social justice educators who have spent their lives shedding light on injustice in its many forms. I especially want to thank all the contributors to this volume, who responded so readily to the call, sharing their thoughts with conviction, sensibility, and sincerity. And to Patty Whang, collaborator extraordinaire, who made the journey with me through all of the twists and turns that come with editing a book of this kind. To my wife, Lisa, whose public life is a testament to standing firm and strong for one's beliefs, to my eldest son, Dion, who has a big heart for all, to my son, Julius, whose strong intellect, integrity, and ethical nature manifests itself in how he cares and helps others, and to my daughter Lia, who has a gracious understanding and compassion for all.

My (Patty) humblest gratitude goes out to Lou for planting the seed that started this whole effort and our co-conspirators who believed enough in this project and us to contribute the essays that make this book everything that it is. May we continue to find ways to provoke more seeing, questioning, caring, and acting for the common good. To my kids, Alexandra and Zachary, who over the years have constantly asked me when I am going to write a book – I say, "here it is" and mahalo to you both and Kalea for giving me reason to work toward a re-imagined world…one that is kinder, gentler, and sustainable. I look forward to seeing the ways in which your lives make this world a better place. To the other members of my ohana, Peter (who so completely shares the joys and challenges of daily life – even if it is a struggle to get him to do Tai Chi), mom and Rich (whose constant love and support has been sustaining), and grandma Clara (who is willing to tell it like it is and provides a refuge in paradise) … thank you for the ways in which you all have allowed me to have a "life of the mind" in between the craziness of kids, animals, house projects, fruit trees, sports, work, and school. I could not have done it without you all.

PREFACE

Do you find it surprising that the aspiration for justice, especially social justice, is simultaneously revered and contested? That is, there are people who passionately advocate both for and against the very idea of working toward a more socially just society. Perhaps most surprising are the detractors. Consider Glenn Beck's advice during his March 2, 2010 radio broadcast, to "… look for the words 'social justice' or 'economic justice' on your church Web site. If you find it, run as fast as you can." Beck went on to add that, "The term 'social justice' has been completely perverted and hijacked by progressives" (http://www.foxnews.com/story/0,2933,589832,00.html). However, as the President of the Southern Baptist Theological Seminary points out, Beck's "verbal grenades" generated far more heat than light, and that Beck's statements and the reactions to them highlight the limitations of public discourse (www.albertmohler.com/2010/03/15/glenn-beck-social-justice-and-the-limits-of-public-discourse/). The "verbal grenade" did provoke limited discourse – riled people up a bit, but did not escalate into hard thinking and deep exploration of social justice, before Beck and the media moved on to the next hot button issue.

Rattling Chains: Exploring Social Justice in Education is the first book to provide an opportunity to intentionally and deeply grapple with the insights, perceptions, and provocations offered by a rich array of prominent and influential voices in the field of education. The first part of the title, *Rattling Chains*, signifies the importance of keeping the issue of social justice reverberating in the minds of readers, while also working to unchain thinking from entrenched beliefs and unchallenged assumptions. More specifically, this collection of essays "shakes and rattles" by providing a variety of vantage points from which to wallow in the complex, tangled, and simultaneously revered and contested notion of social justice. It is hoped that mucking around in the thinking, perspectives, and actions of a variety of educational scholars challenges entrenched beliefs while unearthing provocative insights. Exploring issues of social justice from various standpoints is intended to lead to a more complex understanding of justice that is social, as well as its possibilities, potency, and resultant tensions.

To provide an understanding of the contributors' mindset when writing their essays about social justice, the solicitation sent to potential contributors is provided below.

Last week, my daughter and I attended a Catholic University open house for prospective incoming freshman. We were herded into a large hall to hear about the merits of the University and its program offerings from the President of the University, Dean of Students, Freshman Coordinator, and a host of other staff members. Social justice was mentioned over and over as the core mission of the

University. From the large hall, we were directed to another session where once again the speaker reiterated that social justice undergirds everything done at the University. During the third session, when social justice was brought up again, a parent raised his hand and said, "I've heard you use the term social justice throughout the morning and I would like you to define it for me. When I hear those words it smacks of socialism and I am not willing to send my son to a school that might indoctrinate him in a concept that is contrary to my or our family values. Could you please define the term?" All the presenters swiveled immediately to the Dean of Students hoping that perhaps she could answer the question thoughtfully and insightfully. Embarrassingly, the Dean stumbling for words and clumsily muttered, "It means engagement. You know engagement with the world. That's what it means engagement." This response did not satisfy the parent who cocked a jaundiced eye and gave the Dean a stern, puzzled look. The Dean moved slowly back towards the other presenters and hesitantly said, "If you would like, we can discuss this further, but I am quite busy this morning."

As you might guess, I started answering the question in my own mind, and it certainly was not a one word hurried dismissive response. On the other hand, could I answer the question in a manner that would satisfy this parent's genuine curiosity? Most probably not, as you will note how I wrestle with defining it in the following paragraphs. I then thought that it would be a good idea for this institution and its representatives to be able to articulate a definition of social justice and its importance to them and their mission, and for that matter, for all institutions (including my own) that profess social justice to be a cornerstone of their vision and mission to be able to do the same. This then led to the idea of asking the same question this parent asked at my daughter's orientation to contemporaries of diverse disciplines, perspectives, and social locations and then compile their responses into an edited book. I asked a colleague, Patty Whang, who teaches courses based on social action to help me with the project. We both decided to send out a cover letter with a simple request, as noted below, to colleagues we thought might be interested in addressing this question.

This is a very simple request and it goes like this:

In your own words (citations are fine) answer the questions, "What is social justice" and "why is or isn't it important to you?"

2,500-3,000 word limit; Times New Roman 12 pt. font

Examples from the real world are encouraged to help make points.

Watch out for straying from the point and becoming too esoteric. The purpose of the book is to provide a provocative collection of viewpoints that help push, in a digestible and meaningful way, a consideration of the consensus and contradictions when it comes to a concept enjoying widespread use. The intended audience includes, for example, institutions, organizations, college students, or parents, who are trying to get their minds around a concept that has multiple meanings and interpretations, either because they are committed to social justice or suspicious of it.

Both editors thought it would be a good idea to lay bare their thinking about social justice.

TEETERING ON THE BRINK OF FRUSTRATION: LOU DENTI

Although the answer that was given by the Dean regarding social justice was insufficient, I began to think about her one word *"it's engagement"* definition. Though it was apparent her answer was flippant, she had somewhere along the line learned that social justice meant some sort of engagement. Did she mean individual engagement and action, community engagement against injustice, societal laws to protect citizens against discrimination, or the global interchange between countries around ideologies? As an academic, I found myself pondering these questions, and at the same time, kicking myself for not standing up right then and there to give my take on the meaning of social justice. I could have slowly weighed in from Plato's Republic, to women's suffrage, to America's civil rights movement, to the Catholic churches commitment to fight for the human rights of the oppressed. However, I was timid, afraid to appear erudite or obstreperous, so I stayed silent, biting my tongue, cowardly resolving my dissonance with a shrug and an "Oh well."

Truth be told, I could have and should have spoken up, telling the assembled group of parents that *social justice comes from one's individual deep and abiding moral and ethical conviction to do what is right and just for others so they too can have an opportunity to participate meaningfully in society.*[1] From an individual point of view, one can think about how as a society *individuals are treated with fairness, dignity and respect.* I could have proposed that *social justice is the foundation for social integration by all groups so they are not deprived of full participation in the normal activities of society on the basis of social distinction/class, race, ethnicity, disability, personal habits, appearance, geography.* Furthermore, I could have shared with conviction that *equality of rights and self-respect, so important for a society to achieve its highest ideals, must be the cornerstone of justice for all.* More specifically, I could have invoked the motto E Pluribus Unum: "out of many, one" which expressly advocates for social inclusion in America.

Most likely my explanation would have been perceived as obsequious and boring and readily dismissed by this very harried group of parents as quickly as the dean's quixotic definition of social justice. Here is what I should have and could have said with a degree of assuredness. For me sir, *social justice is simply defined as access; an individual's fundamental right to access everything a society has to offer without fear of reprisal and to be treated fairly with dignity and respect.* For instance, you have red hair (which he did) and if you were not allowed in this room today because of your hair color you would agree that action would be unjust. Now if you are poor, disabled, or have a different color skin and not given the same rights as others you would say that is unjust. Simply because you have red hair,

---

[1] Italics indicate my [L. Denti's] definition of social justice.

you no longer have access to what you undeniably think is your right as a human being. Additionally, there was a sign outside the door in bold letters that you apparently missed – **No Red Hair People Admitted to This Room at Anytime**. I have now made you inferior and everyone else superior, thus reducing your freedom and access: both inalienable rights as a human being. I have given you an ascribed status and you have a place outside the room, where you now belong.

The absurdity of my example highlights my definition of social justice. You sir should not be denied access nor be discriminated against because you have red hair. You should not be cast as an outsider or an "other" or made less worthy because of your appearance or perceived difference. And so it goes for all groups that would like *the freedom and liberty to exercise their rights, to be accepted for who they are, and to participate in the social fabric of society without feeling discriminated against.* When the dean and other university representatives use the phrase social justice today I will, and I hope you will keep this inane example in mind. Whew, what a load off my chest. Would my definition and example dissuaded this gentleman from his position, doubtful, but at least I would have taken responsibility for expressing my point of view about social justice.

Now let me turn to my reason for attending the orientation at a Catholic University. Although this was one the many stops along the college shopping tour, I did want my daughter to learn about social justice and to "do" social justice work, so she not only learns to *accept diversity of race, religion, appearance, social class, but diversity of opinion.* I wanted my daughter to learn that social justice is a concept that evolves through honest and thoughtful discourse and that a university that prides itself on social justice will not denigrate one's differing ideas, but embrace them, even if they may seem antithetical to another's ideas or prevailing definitions of social justice. Wrestling with issues of the day, and then gaining an expanded perception from multiple viewpoints was what I was looking for my daughter. I must admit, like the fellow who questioned the Dean, I wondered if an institution that prides itself on social justice, however, could not define it in layman's terms, was the right fit for my daughter as well.

Even though the definition that I should and could have offered was aimed at the fellow with the red hair, I too, was speculating about how difficult it is to define such a nebulous and imprecise term. For example, if you believe that a women should not have an abortion even when raped, that view, though contrary to mine, would need to be taken seriously in order to determine whether the underpinning of social justice – individual rights, fairness, freedom and equality – of such a position is just or unjust. So you readily see that what justice and fairness means to one person could, as pointed out with the case of abortion and rape, mean the opposite to another person. Implementing social justice policies then becomes even more problematic when religious and sanctity values enter into the picture. As John Rawls would point out, that in this situation the burden of judgment enters full center into the discussion. As reasonable individuals trying to separate religious from political/legal views (the legal right of a woman to chose an abortion whether she was raped or not) becomes difficult at best and trying at most. To ensure that people have the liberty to adopt a point of view or a contrary point of view, we must also then agree that the burden of judgment, as Rawls posits, must be considered. Looking at fairness or justice for women who have been raped from an individual point of view may not be the test for the burden of judgment at the societal level, for that discourse enters into the sphere of, in American society, laws, rights of privacy, and hard fought rights of women who have been discriminated against.

Can one bracket one's liberty of conscience to entertain the notion of the greater good for one in society and the importance of political/legal determinations that support equality, whether conceived as fair or not. So, in the case of a rape victim and not having the right to an abortion, the burden of judgment now rests on the precipice of fairness. If we push fairness over the cliff, we as a society risk the falling headlong into the abyss of unreasonableness: an abyss so evident in and around the world where religiosity or totalitarianism controls thought and reason.

Political and personal liberties, so important in society that values free expression, need never to be contained, for it is in containment that opportunity for cooperation, inclusion, and access lead to less advantage for the marginalized and disenfranchised. Better to talk or argue it out in the public sphere and rely on reasonableness to be the barometer to ensure that equality, fairness, and freedom to express one's views continues to be honored and prized and that tenable persons in a society will continue to search for a common good to support all members of a society without curtailing will and motivation to succeed.

Now I must give my due to noble laureate Friedrich Hayek. For when the fellow with red hair boldly asserted that social justice is just socialism and he did not want his son to be indoctrinated with socialistic thoughts or beliefs, he was begging for comment, not argument. His fear, if I might presuppose, emanated from a deep distrust for anything that might imply leftist liberalism and a diminution of individual liberty, especially if an institution dare impose its economic, political, social, and moral values on a young mind. Hayek, in the *Mirage of Social Justice*, points out that social justice is an empty phrase railing against the imposition of government as intrusive and imposing. Hayek advocated for allowing the forces of the free market to create spontaneous order, not an order compelled upon by the state. According to Hayek, order imposed upon by the state restricts freedom thus creating a climate for socialism. Hayek hypothesized that justice resides in the individual commanded by virtues that impel a person to act in a virtuous manner. Social justice cannot be reified to a unit wherein a congregate of individuals or a society can be deemed just or unjust. I do not think for a moment that this parent was concerned with Catholic morality or doctrine, but was more concerned about liberal teaching and propaganda that was antithetical to his conception of social justice, consequently aligning himself with Hayek, though he may have never read anything by Hayek or had the slightest idea who he was or what he stood for. Hayek, whose writings I respect, but whose ideas I disagree with, was now part of this/my generative dialectic.

My head was wound tight when I left the university orientation that day. I went straight to my dog-eared copy of *The Republic of Plato* to placate and absolve myself from remaining silent and to search for a definition of social justice. Plato believed that justice resides in both the individual and society at large. At the individual level, virtuous behavior means wisdom, courage, moderation and justice: all virtues that underscore goodness. Elevated to a societal level, society takes on a social conscientiousness – working together as a whole towards goodness and harmony.

Nonetheless, Plato's writings, though brilliant, did not soothe my discontent. I also knew invoking Martin Buber, Virgina Satir, Riane Eisler, Alistair McIntyre, Gunnar Myrdal, Max Lerner, Elie Wiesel, Michael Polanyi, Margaret Mead, Victor Frankel, Cornel West and other eminent authors who shaped my early thinking around what it means to be socially conscious, could not give me a way to navigate through the mine field of social justice definitions I now encounter from print, TV, radio, and social media. Social justice for the extreme right has now become synonymous with anti-Americanism sentiments, government take over, and anti-capitalism while the modern left hangs on to organized labor, public welfare, free public education, and services for the most vulnerable in our society. Both sides seem to have polar opposites views and the ideological divide has become so wide, that rants and shouts have replaced dialogue and any hope of understanding or compromise. Knowing this and feeling so beleaguered by the erosion of democracy and civility, I turned to my colleagues to help me define or redefine social justice in the field of education, expand my thinking, enlighten me, and or at the very least, help me ease my mind. Much to my surprise, my colleagues immediately responded to my call; hence the book that is now before you.

Knowing full well this sort of book would be a challenge, I leaned on my colleague, Patricia Whang, who has spent a good deal of her career teaching social justice, to not only partner with me in this endeavor, but to share her deep understanding and connection with social justice work. She was intrigued by the offer, and without hesitation, joined in on this journey. The next part of this introduction will be devoted to her thoughts on social justice and how she has come to her own working definition.

BUDDHISM, SOCIAL JUSTICE, AND THE WORK OF EDUCATORS: PATRICIA WHANG

I am not a Buddhist.

I am, however, a student of Buddhist teachings. My introduction to Buddhist teachings happened almost by happenstance and in a most mundane way. While shopping at Costco a few years ago, I noticed a book by The Dalai Lama (2002), picked it up, started reading and was immediately struck by the insights and provocations. Even after reading just a few pages, I was intrigued by the connections between the Buddhist teachings and the scholarly literature I had been immersing myself in, especially the literature that is committed to transgressive (hooks, 1994, 2003) and/or liberatory (Freire, 2000) education. I bought that book and began exploring the potential synergy between Buddhist teachings and transgressive and libertaory pedagogical practice (Whang, 2007; Whang & Peralta-Nash, 2005). I assert that achieving a more socially just society requires such an education because, we are not socialized to see (especially deeply or critically), question, care, and/or act. Buddhist teachings helps me in my pursuit of understanding the why of many common practices, perspectives, and behaviors, as well as provides the means for seeing, thinking and doing differently. As will be articulated later, such socialization effectively helps to maintain the status quo. I know that it took another fortuitous event to wake me up from the confines of my socialization.

The beginnings of my continuous efforts to awaken from the stupor of my socialization to not see, rarely question, fleetingly care, and definitely not act against the status quo happened, rather ironically, in Auburn Alabama. I say ironically, because Auburn is located in the Bible belt of the deep South where Southern hospitality, genteel manners, and pride in traditions and football reigns supreme. This is not a place one thinks of as radical, revolutionary, or nurturing the will to disrupt the status quo. As a newly minted Ph.D., my first faculty position was in a College of Education at Auburn University. This was an especially invigorating time to be a junior faculty member because it was time of a number of new hires who brought varied understandings and perspectives. I owe my awakening to the patient prodding of three brilliantly provocative colleagues namely Pamela J. Bettis, Nirmala Erevelles, and Kimberly L. King. Together, under the guise of a reading group, we read Jonathan Kozol's (1975) underground classic, *The Night is Long and I am Far from Home.* Reading this hard hitting book and discussing it with my colleagues served to effectively disrupt my narrow preoccupations as an Educational Psychologist and helped me to understand the importance of working toward a world that is kinder, gentler, as well as more aware, curious, and just.

For the current volume, the invited contributors were asked to respond, in 2500 words or less, to the following questions, "What is social justice" and "why is or isn't it important to you?" Respondents were encouraged to use examples from the real world to make points. Providing contributors with such unfettered discursive space was intentional because Lou and I were interested in analyzing the essays for emergent themes and interesting points of divergence that could be used to deepen conversations about and perhaps both wobble and deepen understandings of social justice. That analysis is reflected in the structure of the book. More specifically, though many of the essays contributed to multiple emergent themes, they were placed in the themed section where the insights offered and points made resonated most strongly or were most potent. So, each of the three sections that follow contains an introduction that is intended to provide a frame of reference for exploring the simultaneously revered and contested notion of social justice. Buddhist teachings will serve as that frame of reference. That Buddhist teachings should have a place in a book exploring the terrain of myriad understandings of social justice should not be surprising, given that at the heart of Buddhist teachings is the understanding that all human beings – "… no matter what our situation, whether we are rich or poor, educated or not, of one race, gender, religion, or another, we all desire to be happy and to avoid suffering" (Lama, 2001, p. 4). From this, I think of social justice as a commitment to living in ways that minimizes suffering. Buddhist teachings are helpful in making good on such a commitment because they offer insight into transforming ourselves, our relationships, and our world. More specifically, Buddhist teachings and practices offer concrete tools for achieving greater awareness, understanding, and reflectiveness, as well as insight into how to free oneself from harmful physical, emotional or cognitive (re)actions. Moreover, Buddhist teachings provide concrete advice for nurturing and sustaining caring relationships, whether those relationships are with people near or far, material objects, or the earth.

REFERENCES

Freire, P. (2000). *Pedagogy of the oppressed*. Continuum International Publishing Group.

Hayek, F. A. (1976). Law, Legislation, Liberty, Volume 2: The Mirage of Social Justice. Chicago IL: University of Chicago Press

hooks, bell. (1994). *Teaching to transgress: Education as the practice of freedom*. Routledge.

hooks, bell. (2003). *Teaching community: A pedagogy of hope* (1st ed.). Routledge.

Kozol, J. (1975). *The night is dark and I am far from home*. Boston: Houghton Mifflin.

Lama, T. D. (2001). *Ethics for the new millennium*. Riverhead Trade.

Lama, T. D., & Vreeland, N. (2002). *An open heart: Practicing compassion in everyday life*. Back Bay Books.

Whang, P. A. (2007). The Buddha view: ReVIEWing the instersection of educational psychology and teacher development. In J. Kincheloe & R. Horn (Eds.), *Encyclopedia of educational psychology* (pp. 410-417). Greenwood Press.

Whang, P. A., & Peralta-Nash, C. (2005). Reclaiming compassion: Getting to the heart and soul of teacher education. *Journal of Peace Education*, 79-92.

PATRICIA A. WHANG

SECTION 1: INTRODUCTION

Refusing the Bliss, Embracing the Hurt, and Rocking the Boat

The section introductions are intended to serve as touchstones for considering the insights offered in the essays that compose that section. Touchstones can be helpful, because they provide a point of reference from which to critically evaluate new information or insights, as well as identify missing or underdeveloped ideas. Having a touchstone to return to also reduces the likelihood of getting lost in ideas. A touchstone should not be confused with a millstone, which metaphorically weighs one down and makes movement difficult. Rather, it is hoped that the touchstones will serve as unique and provocative vantage points from which to consider and evaluate the points raised in the essays.

Though many different touchstones could have been chosen, Buddhist teachings are deployed here. This is not about religion, but about spirituality. Perhaps it is necessary to quote the Dalai Lama (2001) at length to establish the appropriateness of such a touchstone for a project on social justice:

> Spirituality I take to be concerned with those qualities of the human spirit – such as love and compassion, patience, tolerance, forgiveness, contentment, a sense of responsibility, a sense of harmony – which bring happiness to both self and others ... the unifying characteristic of the qualities I have described as "spiritual" may be said to be some level of concern for others' well-being ... thus spiritual practice according to this description involves, on the one hand, acting out of concern for others' well-being. On the other hand, it entails transforming ourselves so that we become more readily disposed to do so. To speak of spiritual practice in any terms other than these is meaningless .... My call for a spiritual revolution is thus not a call for a religious revolution .... Rather, it is a call for a radical reorientation away from our habitual preoccupation with self. It is a call to turn toward the wider community of being with whom we are connected, and for conduct which recognizes others' interests alongside our own. (pp. 22-24)

Later the Dalai Lama assures the reader that he is not being simplistic and suggesting that problems of human origin, like wars, crime, violence, corruption, poverty, or social, political, and/or economic injustices can be solved simply by cultivating particular spiritual values. Rather, the point is that "when this spiritual dimension is neglected, we have no hope of achieving a lasting solution" (Lama, 2001, p. 24). Thus, the intentional use of Buddhism as a touchstone provides a longstanding body of teachings to this consideration of what social justice is, why it is important, and how it can be achieved because it pushes us to reVIEW

Louis G. Denti and Patricia A. Whang (eds.), Rattling Chains: Exploring Social Justice in Education, 1–5.
© 2012 *Sense Publishers. All rights reserved.*

ourselves and our relationship to others. This seems to be an appropriate vantage point to consider when pursuing an understanding of justice that is social. As a reminder of the particular touchstone for that section, each of the essays in that section begin with a common phrase in their titles.

The touchstone for this first set of essays, directs our attention to the importance of cultivating both awareness and a willingness to critically examine and question that which appears to be universal, natural, normal, and/or eternal. Hence, the phrase "Working to Awaken" is included in the titles that constitute this section as a reminder of overarching insights that can be distilled from the essays. The Buddhist concept of mindfulness may prove useful here. Mindfulness is at the heart of Buddhist teachings (Hanh, 1999a) and has been described as a quality of mind or learned state of perception (Goldstein, 2003) that keeps one's consciousness alive to the present reality (Hanh, 1999b). It is also necessary for breaking free from habitual responses and/or taken for granted assumptions. Achieving mindfulness requires developing the ability to stay open, curious, and attentive and is important because being fully present in the current moment impacts one's reading of the world and subsequent actions. Chödrön (2008) would add that we need increasing opportunities to experience openness by learning to recognize when we are falling into the habitual or operating on automatic pilot by opening our minds and connecting to where we are. Perhaps these are important considerations when pursuing an understanding of social justice, because without their cultivation, far too many of us are "cocooned" from (Kennedy, 1987), distracted from (Chödrön, 2008) or anesthetized to (Kozol, 1975) the need to act because of our socialization.

A useful concept for exploring this state of affairs is that of ideology. Societies rely on ideologies to serve as social glue and provide road maps that help people to understand how the society works, make decisions, and interact in daily life (Kellner, 1978). Kellner (1978) identifies two different types of ideology. The first, ideology-as-ism, refers to ideas, images, and theories that can stoke a reimagining of how the world could be different and thus mobilize people to social activism. An example is Marxism. As Kellner (1978) further explains, "These ideologies posited a faith in the power of ideas to change consciousness, and a faith in the powers of people to change the world" (p. 44).

The second type, hegemonic ideology, pushes us to examine how we are socialized to accept, without question or criticism, dominant ideas and representations in a given social order (Ayers, 2009; Burbules, 1992; Kellner & Durham, 2001). As Kellner and Durham (2001) explain:

> Ideologies appear natural, they seem to be common sense, and are thus often invisible and elude criticism. Marx and Engels began a critique of ideology, attempting to show how ruling ideas reproduce dominant societal interests serving to naturalize, idealize, and legitimate the existing society and its institutions and values. (p. 6)

Influencing the socialization of others through the naming of the world and the framing of issues is powerful work (Ayers, 2009). Thus, it should come as no surprise that dominant social groups use their resources (e.g., assets, opportunities, and power) to broadly influence the socialization of the masses through controlling the production of cultural artifacts (e.g., magazines, movies, popular music), representations, relations, practices, perspectives, and institutions (Kellner & Durham, 2001). The ability of dominant social groups to exert such control – especially control that is beyond question – means that how the majority of us come to understand the world and our places in it is not neutral or benign, but is infused with the biases, interests, and values of the dominant group so as to further justify and preserve their domination and control. Furthermore, these habits of mind are strong. Thus, great discipline and intentionality are needed to break through the cocoon that the habitual and the automatic creates for us (Chödrön, 2008).

Because schools, as societal institutions, have been described as both "a window and a mirror into any social order .... Our schools show us exactly who we are – the good, the bad, and the ugly – beneath the rhetoric and the self-congratulatory platitudes" (Ayers, 2009, p. 391), they are important sites from which to examine the production and contestation of ideologies. This is important because opportunities to control the production of policies, practices, or values, that characterize the experience of schooling, result in direct opportunities to shape the socialization of participants in that particular institution. And, in terms of how those opportunities have been used, consider Chomsky (1987) who explains that:

> ... education is a valuable mechanism of control, since it effectively blocks any understanding of what is happening in the world. One crucial goal of successful education is to deflect attention elsewhere ... away for our own institutions and their systematic functioning and behavior, the real source of a great deal of violence and suffering in the world. It is crucially important to prevent understanding and to divert attention from the sources of our own conduct, so that elite groups can act without popular constraints to achieve their goals .... (p. 124)

Freire (Kennedy, 1987) underscores Chomsky's assessment of elite groups when he explains that education, as a tool of the powerful, allows the rich to educate the rich to remain rich, while educating the poor to remain poor and to accept their poverty as normal and natural. Achieving these ends is facilitated by an education that "castrates curiosity" or fails to nurture critical and questioning dispositions. Consider how we are further discouraged from seeking awareness and critically questioning when we are told that "curiosity killed the cat," "not to open Pandora's box," "ignorance is bliss," "what you don't know can't hurt you," and to "not rock the boat." Interestingly, Pema Chödrön's (2008) insights push us to consider the ramifications of school days that are jammed with constant worries about assignments, standards, standardized tests, or the minutiae that makes up the day. These preoccupations may serve to keep us self-absorbed, distracted, and cocooned. Social injustices are easier to maintain when people are encouraged to remain unaware of the nature and causes of those injustices (Mercado, 2000; Sensoy & DiAngelo, 2011). If life as we know it seems fine, then calls for social justice may be perceived as exaggerated and/or unnecessary. Thus, the challenge becomes finding a way to break through the ideological impasses that serve to perpetuate the status quo. The essays in this section underscore the need to "work to awaken," as well as provide suggestions as to what that work might look like.

More specifically, the first three essays in this section provide a consideration of the sort of education that will liberate us from the lull of conformity, obedience, and impotency. In the first essay, using Freire's notion of conscientization, *Julio Cammarota* suggests that social justice is about critical consciousness, because it contributes to a sense of agency and trust in the idea that it is possible to actively make the world a better place. Furthermore, he explains the important role that educators should play in helping students develop such consciousness. This is followed by a piece by *Christine E. Sleeter* who uses vignettes to highlight how openness to and awareness of both different perspectives and different lived experiences can nurture the development of critical consciousness and the need for multicultural education. Next, *Deborah Meier and Nicholas Meier* consider the role of controversy in educating citizens fit for a democracy and a more socially just society. Notice how this stands in sharp contrast to an education that "castrates curiosity" and stymies questioning. The authors assert the importance of educators preparing students to be able to productively negotiate controversies as a mean of achieving "fairness." The last three essays in this section challenge the taken for granted. That is, *Jean Moule*, focuses on the roles that unconscious and unintentional bias play in perpetuating societal ills. Drawing from her personal experiences as a teacher educator, activist, and female of color, Moule creates tension around the ease with which many articulate a commitment to social justice. Next, *Nel Noddings* raises for consideration the possibility that efforts to create greater social justice may serve to preserve the status quo at best and at worst may serve to create disadvantage, by taking away choices and/or narrowing opportunities. As such this essay serves as an example of the value in developing a critical and questioning perspective – even towards actions committed with the best of intentions. Finally, *Dudley-Marling* provokes a reconsideration of the assumption that "special" education benefits the students it serves. He does this by demonstrating how shifting perspectives from the problem being a deficit in the identified individuals to the problem being socially constructed, changes the understanding of what needs to happen to make the situation more just. As the author points out, even if done with the best of intentions, working from the wrong perspective could make the situation worse by perpetuating the status quo despite the appearance of doing something to change the situation.

REFERENCES

Ayers, W. (2009). Barack Obama and the fight for public education. *Harvard Educational Review*, *79*(2), 385-395.

Burbules, N. C. (1992). Forms of ideology – Critique: A pedagogical perspective. *International Journal of Qualitative Studies in Education*, *5*(1), 7-17. doi:10.1080/0951839920050103

Chödrön, P. (2008, September). Waking up to your world. *Shambhala Sun*. Retrieved June 20, 2012, from http://shambhalasun.com/index.php?option=com_content&task=view&id=3247&Itemid=0

Chomsky, N. (1987). The manufacture of consent. *The Chomsky Reader* (pp. 121-136). Pantheon.

Goldstein, J. (2003). *One Dharma: The emerging western Buddhism*. HarperOne.

Hanh, T. N. (1999a). *The heart of the Buddha's teaching*. Three Rivers Press.

Hanh, T. N. (1999b). *The miracle of mindfulness: An introduction to the practice of meditation* (1st ed.). Beacon Press.

Kellner, D. M. (1978). Ideology, Marxism, and advanced capitalism. *Socialist Review, 8*(42), 37-65.

Kellner, D. M., & Durham, M. G. (2001). Adventures in media and cultural studies: Introducing the KeyWorks. In M. G. Durham & D. M. Kellner (Eds.), *Media and cultural studies* (1st ed., pp. 1-29). Wiley-Blackwell.

Kennedy, W. B. (1987). Conversations with Paulo Freire on pedagogies for the non-poor. In *Pedagogies for the Non-Poor* (pp. 219-231). Maryknoll, NY: Orbis Books.

Kozol, J. (1975). *The night is dark and I am far from home*. Boston: Houghton Mifflin.

Lama, T. D. (2001). *Ethics for the new millennium*. Riverhead Trade.

Mercado, D. (2000). Introduction. *Chomsky on miseducation* (pp. 1-14). Lanham, MD: Rowman & Littlefield Publishers.

Sensoy, O., & DiAngelo, R. (2011). *Is everyone really equal? An introduction to key concepts in social justice education*. Teachers College Press.

JULIO CAMMAROTA

WORKING TO AWAKEN: EDUCATORS AND CRITICAL CONSCIOUSNESS

In education, social justice is an awareness of conditions by which young people transition through various stages of development to attain critical consciousness. The stages of development most appropriate for this discussion of social justice in education derive from Paulo Freire's (1998) conceptualization of conscientization – the highest level of awareness of structures and conditions influencing one's humanization. Freire (1998, 519 fn1) defines conscientization as a "process in which men, not as recipients, but as knowing subjects, achieve a deepening awareness both of the sociocultural reality that shapes their lives and other capacity to transform that reality." Conscientization is attained by transitioning through social justice conditions – related to the realms of the self, community, and global – leading to a human agency capable of transforming the world. Although conscientization represents the culmination of transitions of awareness, the actual conditions necessary for the transitions are not fully described in Freire's conceptualization. Social justice in education provides a typology to help identify the conditions required to move through various development stages to attain conscientization (Cammarota, forthcoming).

In this essay, I describe the various stages of development leading to conscientization. Each stage will be matched to a corresponding social justice condition in education necessary to move forward toward the highest level of critical consciousness. Social justice in education, as it pertains to human development, comprises an awareness of conditions occurring from the social structures and institutions that either impede or facilitate the agency for personal, community, and global transformation. Thus, social justice in education renders the transition through the stages of consciousness and the attainment of conscientization. The conclusion explores how social justice in education counters the "culture of silence" imposed onto dominated people by the dominant group.

THE LEVELS OF CONSCIOUSNESS

Freire (1970, 1998) asserts that at least three significant types of consciousness (magical, naive, and critical) are apparent throughout the general population, representing successive stages in human development leading to conscientization. The first or lowest stage is termed *magical consciousness* in which people believe God predetermines their fate. They assume they have no control over circumstances and therefore accept that their lot in life is given and immutable.

Louis G. Denti and Patricia A. Whang (eds.), Rattling Chains: Exploring Social Justice in Education, 7–12.
© 2012 *Sense Publishers. All rights reserved.*

Freire (1998, p. 506) states that with the absence of a "structural perception, men attribute the sources of ... situations in their lives either to some super-reality or to something within themselves; in either case to something outside objective reality." When reflecting on the reason for poverty, those with a *magical consciousness* will most likely assert that it is God's will. The danger with this type of consciousness is that oppressed populations will have little motivation to change their status. God determines and fixes reality to the point in which people feel they have no other choice but to accept their subordination. Freire (1998) adds:

> If the explanation for those situations lies in a superior power, or in men's own 'natural' incapacity, it is obvious that their action will not be orientated towards transforming reality, but towards those superior beings responsible for the problematical situation, or toward that presumed incapacity. (p. 506)

The second stage of development, according to Freire, is *naive consciousness* in which people assume that their situation in life is the result of family upbringing and culture. Thus, an individual's success or failure is perceived as directly related to how they have been raised and the kinds of cultural beliefs they have been exposed to while growing up. Freire (1998) claims that *naive consciousness* exists at a higher level than *magical consciousness* because people begin to grasp that human interventions shape reality and not superior beings. However, the myths of the magical level linger on in a *naive consciousness* by perceiving human intervention as an absolute and immutable category that cannot be transformed.

In American society, *naive consciousness* is quite prevalent and informs a dominant explanation for the low academic attainment of students of color. Those embracing this consciousness believe that many students of color fail because they originate from families or cultures that do not value education, resulting in a lack of motivation to succeed in school. In this regard, *naive consciousness* parallels "deficit thinking" (Valencia, 1997) in that failure is understood as a problem of deficiency on the part of the students and their families. In other words, it presumes certain communities lack the "right" family and cultural values for academic success.

The final stage of development is *critical consciousness* and thus represents the attainment of conscientization. Those adhering to this type of consciousness will understand that living conditions derive from social and economic systems, structures, and institutions. God, family, and culture have little to do with the circumstances of one's environment. Rather, it is individual and collective agency, along with the structures that result from that agency, that have the most significant influence over peoples' living situations. God, family, and culture do not directly engender wealth or poverty; structures of privilege, oppression and exploitation do. Freire (2008) asserts, "The more accurately men grasp true causality, the more critical their understanding of reality will be .... Further, *critical consciousness* always submits that causality to analysis; what is true today is not true tomorrow" (p. 39).The primary benefit of *critical consciousness* is that it clarifies that reality is not fixed and immutable but rather the product of human construction. Therefore, if humans create social conditions, they also have the power to alter those conditions. Individuals who attain *critical consciousness*, perhaps the highest stage of human development, feel capable and confident they can change the material conditions of their lives and of those around them.

THE CONDITIONS OF SOCIAL JUSTICE

Establishing an awareness of social justice conditions in education attains conscientization. The conditions pertain to the realms of the self, community, and global. The first and most foundational of the three is the condition of self in positive, healthy terms. Youth, especially black and Latino, often experience socially induced fractures in their identities. The consistent social pressure and aggression they experience simply from being people of color unfairly marks them as intellectually deficient and socially deviant (Smith-Maddox & Solórzano, 2002; Steele, 1997). Negative representations of youth materialize in media productions, government policies, and popular discourses (Haymes, 2003). The extent of these representations saturate the lived social context of youth, and the effect is often a lowering of self-esteem and confidence (Steele, 1997). To reverse this trend, youth must engage in a learning process that heals their social fractures and nurtures positive self-perceptions of their racial/ethnic identities.

An understanding of how to manifest positive conditions for self-representation will help young people move beyond a *magical consciousness* towards critical consciouness. The effect of a *magical consciousness* is the disbelief in one's capability for change; there is the perception that someone beyond the individual is controlling his or her destiny or he or she has little to no agency. This perception leads to a negative, downtrodden understanding of one's image and moreover, one's potential in the world. An awareness of the condition of one's image and how it influences the perception of one's potential begins a process of transformation. If a young person starts to perceive him or herself in a more positive light, then he or she will start to realize that someone or some being is not controlling his or her fate. The young person sheds the magical consciousness to recognize that he or she has more input and control over his or her potential.

The attainment of positive self-conditions requires building greater awareness of community conditions that impede healthy development (Ginwright & Cammarota, 2002). The condition of the community, the second in the set, derives from an understanding of how social and economic forces in young people's lived context contribute to the fracturing of their identities. Consistent exposure to austere poverty, dysfunctional schools, police harassment, and environmental degradation will lead to unhealthy outcomes but also lowered self-esteem, confidence, and misrecognition of capacities. Therefore, learning and development processes must not only heal the *self* but also focus on healing the community and palliating those social and economic toxins that poison young people's hope for the present and future.

An awareness of the social and economic conditions will help young people to surpass naïve *consciousness* by understanding that obstacles impeding progress often derive from structures, systems, or institutions and not from personal incapacity. Lack of opportunities or inferior education prevents young people from advancing socially and economically. Once young people realize that the absence of opportunities is the culprit instigating their low status, they stop blaming themselves or their family and culture for their circumstances. They begin to analyze the structures rendering opportunities to see how and what ways they experience external impediments to their well being. By identifying these impediments, young people can address and thus overcome them to change the course of their lives.

Personal hope is elevated through feeling compassionate for those who experience suffering, yet exist beyond the individual's immediate community (Ginwright & Cammarota, 2002). The third and last in the set, the condition of the global constitutes the final stage of consciousness and thus conscientization formed through social justice in education. An awareness of global conditions involves understanding how oppression affects the lives of others while contributing to social justice practice that counters this oppression. Showing empathy for people who suffer from pressures impalpable in one's personal context builds a sense of compassion that aspires to bettering the world for all. Once young people feel they can contribute to improving the lives of others, they become compassionate and thus confident about cultivating positive changes in their own lives. Young people will fail to understand how to affect individual changes if they miss the opportunity to demonstrate compassion for human suffering that occurs peripheral to them.

By understanding that oppression exists on a global scale and affects those beyond one's community, an individual can attain the highest level of *critical consciousness*. Acknowledging and knowing how other people suffer who live outside of one's social context requires a sophisticated degree of analysis and thus understanding of how structures foment oppression. Although the contexts maybe different, analysis of a distant and unfamiliar situation can still provide the analytical tools to examine and comprehend one's own circumstances. It is through this global study of oppression that young people attain the analytical insights for developing a *critical consciousness*.

SOCIAL JUSTICE IN EDUCATION

The attainment of conscientization through practices that establish the conditions for positive reflections and involvements in the realms of the self, community, global constitutes social justice in education. These practices may include educational work that analyzes the structures and institutions that fracture identities while generating cultural productions that repair them. For instance, students can study how certain media institutions unfairly represent young people of color. To counter the negative portrayal, they can create their own media products offering more positive representations. Social justice practices may also proffer opportunities to increase young people's community engagement. Thus, students may examine poverty to understand negative conditions in their communities. Their examination could lead to a campaign to raise minimum wages in their cities or towns. To adopt a positive global perspective, students may interact with refugees and migrants and ensure they receive the same rights and benefits as "native" citizens.

These social justice practices are meant to counter what Freire (1998) calls the "culture of silence." According to Freire (1998):

> understanding the culture of silence presupposes an analysis of the dependence as a relational phenomenon that gives rise to different forms of being, of thinking, of expression, those of the culture of silence and those of the culture that 'has a voice. (p. 503)

Dominant groups impose a "silence" over dominated people by not allowing them opportunities to express their ideas, thoughts, or beliefs. Therefore, in the broadest sense of culture (i.e. societal culture), most human productions of any social bearing and influence originate from the dominant group. These productions become so hegemonic that the dominated people begin to accept them as their own. Their true needs and interests exit in long periods of silence in which change becomes almost impossible to attain. Only by breaking the silence can dominated people seek the changes that will lead to their liberation. Social justice in education is a way to break through the silence and start the process of elevating the voices, concerns and accurate representations of dominated people.

EXTENSION QUESTIONS/ACTIVITIES

1. Cammorata says that social justice in education, as it pertains to human development, comprises an awareness of conditions occurring from the social structures and institutions that either impede or facilitate the agency for personal, community, and global transformation. How does one attain the awareness he speaks about in his essay?

2. Standing up against a social injustice (often perpetuated by a dominant group) breaks the "silence" posited by Paulo Freire leading to a sense of empowerment and transformation. Have you broken the silence and stood up against an injustice? Explain when, where, and what happened.

3. Cammarota posits that showing empathy for people who suffer from pressures impalpable in one's personal context builds a sense of compassion that aspires to bettering the world for all. Respond to this statement by writing your thoughts down in a stream of consciousness manner-whatever comes to mind. You can draw your thoughts out, bullet points, narrative style, rap, etc. Make sure to reflect your ethnic, linguistic, and cultural background when responding.

REFERENCES

Cammarota, J. (forthcoming). From hopelessness to hope: Social justice pedagogy in urban education and youth development. *Urban Education*.

Freire, P. (1970). *Education for critical consciousness*. New York: Continuum.

Freire, P. (1998). Cultural action and conscientization. *Harvard Educational Review, 68*(4), 499-522.

Ginwright, S., & Cammarota, J. (2002). New terrain in youth development: The promise of a social justice approach. *Social Justice, 29*(4), 82-95.

Haymes, S. (2003). Toward a pedagogy of place for black urban struggle. In. S. May (Ed.), *Critical multiculturalism: Rethinking multicultural and antiracist education* (pp. 42-76). London and Philadelphia: Falmer Press.

Smith-Maddox, R., & Solorzano, D. G. (2002). Using critical race theory, Paulo Freire's problem-posing method, and case study to confront race and racism in education. *Qualitative Inquiry, 8*(1), 66-84.

Steele, C. (1997). A threat in the air: How stereotypes shape intellectual identity and performance. *American Psychologist, 52*(6), 613-629.

Valencia, R. (1997). *The evolution of deficit thinking: Educational thought and practice*. Washington, DC: Falmer Press.

Julio Cammarota
University of Arizona

CHRISTINE E. SLEETER

WORKING TO AWAKEN: SEEING THE NEED FOR MULTICULTURAL EDUCATION

To me, multicultural education and social justice education mean much the same thing, probably because I have always linked multicultural education with its roots in the Civil Rights movement. In its inception, multicultural education grew from the work of African American educators and parents who challenged the idea that their homes and communities are culturally deficient and their children lacking in learning ability. "Ethnic education" became "multicultural education" as multiple groups pressed for similar changes in school practices in a quest for education rights. The term social justice came along later, partly because of the way in which many people interpret multicultural education. That is, as interpretations of multicultural education evolved, they did not include the importance of collective struggles for rights, justice, and equity.

Consider the following scenario, which is a fictionalized representation of many conversations I have been part of. When I tell White people who do not know me that my work is in multicultural education, I often end up in a conversation that goes something like the following:

White parent: What kind of work do you do?

Me: I prepare teachers in multicultural education.

White parent: Oh! My daughter's school has wonderful cultural celebrations! Every year they have an international festival in which each classroom represents a country. There is food, dancing, singing – it's a colorful event. We like the school because of things like their multicultural programs, but we worry because so many of the students' parents don't seem to care about education, you know, so sometimes my daughter isn't challenged as much as I'd like.

Me: What do you mean? The parents have told you they don't care?

White parent: (a bit uncomfortable) Well, of course not. But there are a lot of immigrant kids who don't know English very well, and their parents have menial jobs, so content just has to be watered down for them because they don't know much. And some kids have parents who are in jail. The school is close to a bad neighbourhood. We've thought about moving, but so far I've had good luck requesting my daughter's teachers, so she has been able to be grouped with other good kids. And I like how the school's multicultural programs are helping her develop an open mind, you know. It's so beautiful when children get along with each other.

Louis G. Denti and Patricia A. Whang (eds.), Rattling Chains: Exploring Social Justice in Education, 13–17.
© 2012 *Sense Publishers. All rights reserved.*

By this point in the conversation, I'm either speechless, or weighing how much time it would take for me to try to dislodge almost every assumption this parent has made. This parent sees culture as something that comes from somewhere else, to be brought out and tasted every now and then. To her, "multicultural" means sampling several cultures that are understood in this way, for the purpose of broadening children's experience and making school fun. At the same time, she sees the students of color, immigrant students, and students from low-income homes as lacking a foundation for learning, caring parents, and cultural resources. Like this fictionalized parent, White people often use code words like "bad neighborhood" to refer to communities of color, and "good kids" to refer to other children like their own. Assuming that schools are doing their best to serve everyone, but that some children (like hers) are better equipped to learn, the parent uses her own power to make sure her child has access to the best teachers. There is little evidence that the parent is aware that other parents most likely want the same for their children but face barriers she does not face. The parent in question also does not seem to recognize how she participates in a system that unfairly benefits people like herself at the expense of people of color and people who are poor. The term "multicultural" led this parent to a set of assumptions that sidestep consideration of equity and social justice. However, telling her that I prepare teachers for social justice would likely evoke yet another set of assumptions to challenge.

Let me explain. I had not begun to think about what social justice might mean until I was a young adult, and had some experiences that challenged many of my own prior assumptions. As a child, I frequently thought about what is fair in how people treat each other, but my conception of fairness generally revolved around interpersonal issues. For example, if a friend said something disparaging about another person, I often questioned whether the comment was fair to the other person. I recall occasions in which a White person (such as an older relative) said something disparaging about a Black person, and I recall questioning the speaker on the basis of not knowing the other person. Making assumptions about another person is not fair; denying another person a chance is not fair.

But social justice is more than that.

When I was about 22, having moved from the predominantly White small towns where I had lived previously to inner-city Seattle, I found myself face to face with new realities. One of those realities was racial housing segregation. I vividly recall an incident in which an African American friend wanted to move and was looking for a place to live. Having been somewhat aware of the Civil Rights movement, I assumed that housing segregation had been made illegal, so I was taken aback when my friend described his experiences, which included doors not being opened to him, places advertised as available suddenly being rented, and so forth. As he described his experiences, I believed him because I knew him. Over time, in many situations like this, as I listened to and learned about racism as African Americans experienced it, my understanding of fairness acquired dimensions that had not been there before.

First (at least, first in my learning curve), I began to question who has the power to define reality. As I had grown up, I tacitly accepted White professional class adults as the legitimate definers of reality. But as it became clear that my African Americans friends, and many students I was teaching, experienced a different reality than I had grown up with, I began to tie the narratives people tell to the realities they live. In the process, rather than dismissing what people say who might have less education, less money, or less status than I do, I began to take people's stories as a jump-off point for learning. I also began to critique all sorts of media, including textbooks, television, news, and so forth, to identify the viewpoint and context being expressed.

Second, I began to see the systematic nature of discrimination. For example, when I was in high school, my mother commented that she was glad my school used a tracking system because it gave me and other "college prep" students access to the best teachers. At the time, I remember thinking that this kind of system did not seem fair to those who were not "college prep." Ten years later, as a high school learning disabilities teacher in Seattle, I began to realize that tracking routinely gave the White students from professional class backgrounds access not only to the best teachers but also to the best preparation for college, while students of color and students from working class backgrounds ended up in the "general" or vocational tracks. I also began to suspect that the category of learning disabilities served as a tool for White professional class parents to define their own low-achieving children as smart (on the basis of an IQ test required for identification), thus removing them from other non-White low-achievers (Sleeter, 1986).

Third, I gradually began to connect various forms of difference and discrimination. For example, as my consciousness was developing regarding sexism, women of color were making it clear that White women and women of color experience sexism differently because of racism (Albrecht & Brewer, 1990; Hull, Scott & Smith, 1993). For instance, the highly disproportionate imprisonment of Black and Latino men forces Black and Latino women to think about marriage, family, and work on somewhat different terms than is the case with White women. As another example, the disproportionate overrepresentation of students of color in special education prompts questions regarding connections between racism and disability.

Multicultural education, as an outgrowth of the Civil Rights movement, challenges those systems of discrimination while affirming the diverse identities, points of view, cultural backgrounds, and historical experiences of diverse peoples. Challenging injustices involves collective work that raises consciousness and is directed toward unfair laws, practices, and taken-for-granted ways of doing things, as well as belief systems that support what is unfair. In education, this means challenging patterns like low academic expectations that students of color routinely experience, and tracking and grouping practices that privilege students from White and professional class backgrounds. It also means creating new processes, such as inclusive curricula, inclusive approaches to teaching, ways of connecting schools and communities that do not rely solely on parents coming into the school on the school's terms.

So why the term social justice? What does that term add? Let's drop in on another semi-fictional conversation. This time I am explaining to some teachers how anti-racism, anti-sexism, and other challenges to oppression connect.

Me: What I mean by multicultural education can be called anti-racism, since it directly challenges systemic racism in education and the larger society. Let's take the textbooks you are currently using. Whose point of view predominates?

Teacher 1: When I counted the representation of people in this literature text, I realized that most authors are White, and most main characters are White, even though there are a few authors, main characters, and settings, that represent other groups. If teaching the worldview of White people is so institutionalized that most Whites don't even recognize it as a point of view, that's racism.

Teacher 2: That's racism, but what about sexism? Most of the authors are male, and most of the characters are occupy pretty traditional sex roles.

Me: Multicultural education challenges sexism as well. It challenges any form of discrimination and oppression, including heterosexism.

Teacher 3: So if its anti-racist, and anti-sexist, and anti-heterosexist, and anti-classist …

Me: Yes, and anti-ableist.

Teacher 3: Then what do you stand *for*? I see what you stand against, but how do you name what you stand *for*?

Me: Ah, good question. What I stand for is justice for everyone. But what's complicated about it is that not one of us can determine what is just for everyone, because to do that would be to assume that one's own point of view is correct for everyone. Instead, what is needed is dialog in which people with different life experiences learn to work out ways of living and doing things that work for all of us.

Ultimately, I view social justice as a moral stance on behalf of human rights. Social justice recognizes the systemic nature of inequalities, assumes that people know and can name their own reality and needs better than anyone else, regardless of how poor or disabled they might be, and assumes that people can learn to work dialogically and collaboratively with others. Maybe the term "social justice" will not be as easily transformed to mean something comfortable that doesn't really change anything, as the term "multicultural education" has been.

EXTENSION QUESTIONS/ACTIVITIES

1. Have you found yourself in a situation where social justice is neutralized or simplified like the interaction between the white parent and the author? How have you responded or how do you respond in these situations without patronizing, proselytizing, or becoming so frustrated that you walk away or demonstrate your disapproval with a haughty look or a jaundiced eye? Explain.

2. In what ways does multiculturalism and social justice overlap for you? Where do both terms diverge? Create some sort of graphic to display where multiculturalism and social justice overlap or seem to be different. Then write a short narrative or jot down some bullet points to explain your thoughts.

3. Thinking about the groups you are member of, which ones have the strongest influence on how you see and understand the world?

REFERENCES

Albrecht, L., & Brewer, R. (Eds.) (1990). *Bridges of power: Women's multicultural alliances.* Santa Cruz, CA: New Society Press

Hull, G. T., Scott, P. B., & Smith, B. (1993). *But some of us are brave: All the women are White, all the Blacks are men: Black women's studies.* New York: The Feminist Press.

Sleeter, C.E. (1986). Learning disabilities: The social construction of a special education category. *Exceptional Children, 53,* 46-54.

Christine E. Sleeter
Emeritus, CSU Monterey Bay

DEBORAH MEIER AND NICHOLAS MEIER

WORKING TO AWAKEN: IMPLICATIONS FOR TEACHING FROM A SOCIAL JUSTICE PERSPECTIVE

Two kindergarteners are squabbling at their desk when the teacher comes over. One of them says to the teacher, "It's not fair, she took all the red ones!"

In a teacher education course, in discussing that while "race" is not a biological category, it is still important to collect data using racial categories so we can recognize where social injustices exist. A student argues that collecting and using this data only further perpetuates social stereotypes, and is thus a poor strategy.

"Teacher, Why aren't we celebrating Columbus Day?" "It's hard to celebrate a man who led to the genocide of many Native Americans," says the teacher. "But if Columbus hadn't come here, I wouldn't be here, and we would not have the spread of the constitutional democracy that America created."

According to Dewey (1944) all societies educate the ruling class to be able to make the important decisions for the society. And in a democracy, he pointed out; all citizens are members of the ruling class. It is this purpose of schooling that we wish to focus this article on – for students to learn the ability to engage meaningfully in the important decisions that affect their lives as members of a democratic society.

These three vignettes illustrate a few of the various themes and issues underlying a discussion of what it means to teach from a social justice perspective. As the first vignette suggests, humans seem to be born with almost instinctual interest in fairness, even if often from a self-centered perspective (it's fair as long as I get more). Implied in the term social justice is that we go beyond a self-centered perspective to concern ourselves with "fairness" for all. Therefore what does it mean for us as educators to explore fairness with students, complexifying it, while also keeping alive that passion for it?

The second vignette raises the issue of individual versus social responsibility for creating "fairness" and justice. What are the controversies around attempts to legislate equality and correct inequities through social intervention?

The third deals with the ornery fact that everything has trade-offs. Any issue, any controversy implies a trade-off; we gain this, but we lose that. Columbus massacred natives, but his voyages were the beginning of opening the world to new trade and exploration, of material goods and ideas, across continents that previously had little contact with each other. The list of possible themes could go on and on.

Louis G. Denti and Patricia A. Whang (eds.), Rattling Chains: Exploring Social Justice in Education, 19–26.
© 2012 *Sense Publishers. All rights reserved.*

When confronted with issues such as these vignettes illustrate, we need to consider how to respond. Such questions are inescapable no matter what or how we teach. Our responses will inevitably reflect our values and beliefs. If we do not acknowledge our own personal agendas, we cannot tackle being "fair" in regards to other agendas. Some on the Right accuse self-proclaimed social justice educators of having an underlying agenda – to teach students to hate America, the West, or their own government. Some on the other side of the political spectrum believe it is their task to expose the truth about the evils of our government, both past and present, and thus to help instigate radical change. Still others argue that we should do neither: "just the facts ma'am," no interpretation that goes beyond the evidence.

The idea that schooling in a democratic society can avoid taking a stand is questionable. Democracy has a stake in a certain cast of mind and spirit that requires years of preparation and training so that these become "habits" of heart and mind. It is counter-productive to subsidize a form of schooling that requires us to pretend that we are neutral about democracy, the Constitution, etc. The focus on reasoned discourse is itself a value, as is the capacity to imagine alternate perspectives, or the nature of acceptable evidence, and assumptions about causality. These intellectual "virtues" – which we have called habits of mind – are intentional, some even "unnatural." These habits encourage certain forms of public inquiry and behavior. They rest on respect for open-mindedness, skepticism and empathy – which some may view with suspicion. Social Justice educators argue that such a stance toward education is required for a democratic society.

Those on all ends of the political spectrum claim they are for Justice. Of course, there is always room for disagreement once we get into particulars. However, what distinguishes *social* justice is the emphasis on "social." The United States has an equally, if not more powerfully, long strong tradition of individualism. We often speak of individual rights, self-reliance, and rugged independence. The belief in personal destiny and making one's own future is strong. "You can grow up to be whatever you want to be," and "pull yourself up by your bootstraps" are common phrases of an American belief system. However, social justice implies that injustice is often done, not to individuals, but to social groups. To Conservatives, the idea that justice may occur due to one's status in a particular social group regardless of individual merit, smacks of liberal egalitarianism, and is contentious. Such a perspective also overlaps with controversies about identity politics that have raged over the past decades.

The political Right is skeptical of the term social justice at this moment in America, not because they are against justice, or believe that extreme inequities are good, but because "we liberals" have owned it as ours. In fact, in Deborah's youth the phrase social justice was a term she associated with Catholicism and religious belief. Many Conservatives believe that interfering politically to correct social injustices makes things worse – that in fact such interventions may be the cause of the problem. They might argue that morality should be left, as most things should, to voluntary institutions. The "market place" of freedom and liberty will take care of social justice. It is from a guru of the Right, Friedrich Hayek (1976) that the following is taken, "I am certain nothing has done so much to destroy the juridical safeguards of individual freedom as the striving after the mirage of social justice."

Michael Novak (2000), in his defense of Hayek, claims that social injustice, as we define it, cannot exist because justice is a moral term and only individuals can be moral. Since social justice is about injustices done by "society" or its institutions, it has no meaning. "Institutional racism" would, we thus presume, be a concept that Novak and Hayek would reject, while most on the left embrace it. For example, consider the claim that:

> "High unemployment" or "inequality of incomes" or "lack of a living wage" are cited as instances of "social injustice." Hayek goes to the heart of the matter: social justice is either a virtue or it is not. If it is, it can properly be ascribed only to the reflective and deliberate acts of individual persons. Most who use the term, however, ascribe it not to individuals but to social systems. (Novak, 2000)

Such classical market economy defenders see the economy not as a human invention, but as a natural force. To say that the economy or market is unfair is akin to saying that it was unfair that one place had more rain than another. To interfere with the natural process of the "invisible hand" of the market undermines "nature" and depends on a far more imperfect dependence on human virtue.

In contrast, those who use the term social justice, do believe, that laws, societies, or institutions can be unjust. Even nature can lead to a lack of justice if society does not deal with the "unfairness" of the consequences of natural phenomenon – droughts, volcanoes, earthquakes, etc. This view may beg the question of whether ill intention is required. If an action, policy or law has the effect of creating or sustaining inequities, then it is socially unjust. Not to act to change a social injustice is therefore a lack of virtue on the part of those individuals and social groups not working for such change. Even if injustices are not always created by the actions of an individual, individual humans are responsible for the impact of unjust public policy. Therefore, to work for social justice is to work for policies and laws that are more likely to result in the equitable distribution of power and resources. When examining such inequities, we notice patterns – non-randomness – in which some groups have more and some have less access to society's power and resources. Social Justice educators seek to expose the young to such patterns, to explicitly confront youngsters in schools with the impact of their own self-interests on others.

While rhetorically everyone agrees the 21st century requires critical thinkers, our schools appear uncomfortable letting students examine critically anything meaningful. Instead, we make the claim that our form of democracy rests upon a citizenry educated to treat their fellow citizens with the respect they wish for themselves. We argue for a democracy that presumes that citizens are in a position to engage in the debates over important decisions that affect their future and have a say in such decisions, when they virtually never see or engage in such practices during schooling, is absurd. In fact, even that a debate exists is mostly hidden from the curriculum.

Gerald Graff (1992) some years ago during the debate about the "common core," argued that what schools must do is "teach the debate" itself, challenging students to explore various perspectives, maybe focused a little more on exposing the less publicized facts under the assumption that the views of the status quo already so permeate our schooling and general media, that a form of "affirmative action" regarding ideas and information is needed.

Learning to debate "the debate" is perhaps, as Graff argues, our best stance. It provides the tools and the language for entering into the critical discourse about the good society with respect for alternate views, and a sound understanding of one's own view, while being open to the possibility of being wrong. It is precisely such habits that as social justice educators we seek to imbed in our future adult citizens. Such skepticism may itself be controversial among many of the families public schools serve. However, should that interfere with an obligation in a democracy to insist on doing so, even when it comes to abhorrent views – starting in schools? Can the Bill of Rights make sense without confronting difficult ideas?

Part of our task as educators is to select those issues that are most critical to preserving and extending democracy. As teachers we are considering all of this given limited time and resources, having to meet and consider multiple purposes and possible mandates; we are not making the decisions in a vacuum. We must weigh multiple priorities against each other in the real day-to-day act of teaching. What "to cover" is as important as what "not to cover" in the reality of school time. This does not apply only to social studies teachers, or to the teaching of literature. It crops up as well in science and the arts and even in mathematics!

Unless we are going to just read from script that someone else gives us, we as teachers are confronted constantly with what and how to present what we plan to teach. Each of these decisions implies certain beliefs about how people learn and the purpose of the education. And actually even to use a script is a decision to, with the same implications.

I (Nicholas) deal with making decisions about what to present almost daily. A recent example is when I discussed the achievement gaps in K-12 education. While the various achievement gaps in education are pretty much commonly accepted as fact (though even there, the magnitude and what constitutes the best evidence of that gap is contentious), what is not agreed upon is the explanation for that gap. Explanations for that gap range from genetic or cultural to blaming those in power for purposely keeping oppressed groups down and much in between. I have to decide which claims to present, decide how I will present those claims, as well how much time and importance to put on the topic at all. Whatever decision I make has implications for what the students of my course will know about the topic. If another professor taught the course, they would make different decisions than I made regarding each of these.

While, I, as a professor, in theory I might want my students to read a wide variety of views and delve deeply into the evidence. In reality I have limited time with my students, and only so much that I can expect them to read. I might decide to give them a view, that given my expertise, I believe to be both more accurate than, and alternative to, what they are likely to be exposed to otherwise. I believe that affording students an opportunity to explore other points of view that may be contrary to their own, creates a more level playing field upon which students can explore their own ideas. I see such decisions, as an effort at restoring some of that needed balance. Through challenging ad hominem assumptions students often come to realize that their angle of vision may be myopic. Broadening their thinking around a topic or issue gives rise to seeing and embracing a bigger far more complex picture.

In the studying of various historical periods, the essential question for the ninth grade humanities curriculum at Central Park East Secondary School was "Is justice always fair?" From this came further questions: Why do we argue that the law is "blind?" Does fairness necessitate "equality" among all? Does it disregard age? Does it take into account expertise, or one's specific relevance to the issue involved? Do we take into account "consequences" or just equality of process? Is it "fair" to exclude people of a certain age from having full democratic rights? By what right? Ditto of course for all the other "excluded" peoples, such as immigrants or convicted criminals.

In teaching there is always a tension between "coverage" and depth. There is also the question of preparing students with enough background information to enter the debate intelligently. During that discussion, is there a place for the teacher to present his/her own view, or is the teacher's role simply that of facilitator? Does the answer depend on the age of the students? The type of class? Can we pretend that our views are just one of many in the classroom? For students who disagree does it open up their minds or close them – feeling impotent to confront the views of an authority whose expertise and articulateness they cannot match?

We do not need to create balance of views in all our classes – although we need to acknowledge and expose students to minority as well as dominant views – since we are trying to redress an imbalance that exists outside school. It is a risky but tenable position that open discourse broadens our students' minds – so that as our niece/granddaughter said of one professor, "I could feel my mind expanding."

Schooling in a democracy is at heart teaching the young how to exercise judgment. If there were only one "truth," judgment would be irrelevant, and democracy unnecessary. Our standardized high stakes testing system reinforces this notion that there can be only one correct response. Yet both schooling and the mass media encourage the young to assume that the only alternative to right answers are wrong ones. We argue that what for of education one receives will influence that development of moral reasoning, one that instead of focusing on right answers, focuses on getting students to learn bout, ask and engage in the debates about the important questions that matter to them and society; the one's that have no right answers. If they do not see this and practice this from an early age, it is unlikely to become a habit of mind.

Perhaps in exclaiming "It's not fair!" very young children are expressing the most neutral and apolitical root of justice. It is not clear whether this early complaint is culturally "taught" or universal. Nonetheless, how we respond to it is surely relevant to its development. In Jean Piaget's discussion of moral stages, he suggests that our concept of fairness has a certain natural progression, which relates to the increasing capacity to hold varied views at the same time, to "play" with perspectives. This playfulness enters not only the oral realm but also the scientific, judicial, mathematical, artistic realms, when we ask such questions as: What if? Supposing that? But Piaget acknowledges that not all humans move to the more sophisticated stages of this development.

Especially in times of crisis, many Americans worry whether students are being taught, under the guise of critically thinking, to undermine "patriotism" and love of one's country. Many citizens suspect that schools are run by "elites" bent on undermining the authority of parents or Church. A friend of Nicholas', who taught fourth grade in a progressive two-way bilingual school, related an issue that arose in her class. She had taught these nine year olds about what had been done to Native Americans during the European settlement of the US and about what had been done to people of color during slavery and of the struggle to undo our racist past. When one of her students got visibly upset, she probed and discovered that this student felt she was asking her to be anti-White. This teacher had to ask herself whether the way she was teaching about these social injustices, both past and current, is intended to confront those with a European heritage, with the goal of creating self-hate? Is there a certain age level when such topics are okay? Or is there some way at any age-level that we need to confront our past without it backfiring on us? Conversely is there a way to discuss controversial issues, and not whitewash the truth while still encouraging students to have an allegiance to their own country and their own heritage? Or are we neutral – teach the brutal facts and let the consequences take care of themselves?

As we mentioned earlier, we respond generally by falling back on one of three positions: Tell the story in a way that encourages patriotism, or conversely radical activism. Tell the story in its age appropriate fullness, warts and all, while also building allegiance to one's country. Or third, present "all sides" and let students feel and believe whatever – it is not our job to build allegiance, or not. Or we try to combine them.

To avoid this, schools have historically either ignored negative aspects of our country's historical past, or put them in the light of past actions that have now been overcome in the inevitable march of progress. One can even teach them as myths, not to be taken as literal historical truths, but serving to unite people around shared values.

In contrast is the view that such myths do more harm than good. In his book *Lies My Teacher Told Me*, Loewen (2007) documents many of the ways that our high school history textbooks whitewash our past with chapter and verse. In the more "ancient" past – 1940s-1950s – the notion of the arc of human progress from the ancient Middle East to modern America was the larger narrative within which we were taught to absorb all the bumps along the road, everything else is a sidebar to this main story of inevitable progress.

One of the reasons for the contemporary focus on social justice is because many of us have come to the conclusion that even well intentioned myths, such as those articulated by Loewen, leave us unprepared to confront modern problems. Emphasizing the positive aspects of European history, while neglecting other histories, whitewashes the past and current realities of social injustices experienced by many. Most detrimental of all, it silences genuine inquiry into difficult issues.

There needs to be a place for students to hear other perspectives and develop their own. Those who have the most to gain from maintaining the status quo are the very people who own the mass media They have the money to promote their views through commercial uses of the media, by deciding what shows are "airable" on network television (including "public" television), and even inordinate influence about what makes it into our adopted textbooks and curriculum. Hence, schools need to be a place as free as they realistically can be to explore truths.

Even if we draw the broadest definition of our task as educators – with close attention to avoiding forms of "brainwashing" there are dilemmas. Even such dilemmas need to be part of the professional life of the school and of the larger school and community discourse.

It is not our intent to give you our answers to all the questions raised in this article, although we have surely not kept our agenda secret. Since there is no way to deal with controversy that does not itself potentially create controversy, we need to explore over and over why democracy, at its heart, presumes controversy and is built upon the premise that controversy is healthy. If so, why not introduce this in schools – if and as we also explore the controversial imbalance between the powers of the adults and the students within our classrooms. For in discussing democracy, we are also exploring, in various academic disciplines, the role of authority and power, hardly easy topics to discuss with the young, but nevertheless essential to our shared future.

Besides, young people love controversy, a good argument, digging beneath, and uncovering. It is precisely at that moment when kids get truly excited that many of us, as teachers, get worried. We've hit a button; we're in vulnerable terrain. But isn't that what it is all about?

EXTENSION QUESTIONS/ACTIVITIES

1. Michael Novak claims that social injustice, as we define it, cannot exist because justice is a moral term and only individuals can be moral. Since social justice is about injustices done by "society" or its institutions, it has no meaning. Jot down some of your thoughts about Novak's claims. How does his claim fit with your personal and professional life? Turn to a partner or form a small group and discuss your thoughts.

2. Does social justice depend on the far more imperfect dependence on human virtue? Try to ferret out the difference between virtue and social justice. Can you have one without the other? For example does social justice require integrity, empathy, tolerance, and kindness-virtuous behavior or does it stand on its own as a construct with a specific definition, valence, and direction. Divide a piece of paper in half like a hot dog and one side put the term social justice and on the other virtue. Try to discern the difference. Draw lines to similarities or overlaps. Form a small group of four and share your thoughts.

3. Define democracy in one powerful sentence. Does your definition include social or justice? If yes, explain why. If no, explain why not.

REFERENCES

Dewey, J. (1944). *Democracy and education.* New York: Macmillan.

Graff, G. (1992). *Beyond the culture wars: How teaching the conflicts can revitalize American education.* New York: W.W. Norton.

Hayek, F. A. v. (1976). *Law legislation and liberty. Vol. 2, The mirage of social justice.* [S.l.]: Routledge.

Loewen, J.W. (2007). *Lies my teacher told me: Everything your American history textbook got wrong.* New York: New Press.

Novak, M. (2000, December). Defining social justice. *First Things,* 11-13.

Deborah Meier
New York University

Nicholas Meier
California State University Monterey Bay

JEAN MOULE

WORKING TO AWAKEN: HIGH ROAD TO ACTION OR LOW ROAD TO CONSCIENCE SALVING

Essay: A short analytical interpretive prose dealing with a particular topic, especially from a personal and unsystematic viewpoint.

I have noted with great detail and compelling evidence, the role of unconscious bias and unintentional racism in the workings of our schools and institutions (Moule, 2009). In this essay I would like to connect my understanding of unconscious bias and unintentional racism more fully to what I see as the undermining of many of our efforts towards social justice in teacher education.

Beginning with details on our college of education's efforts towards social justice I will move to our professional grappling around our differing perspectives. On a more personally reflective level, for the reader, I will articulate key components of racial identity development and unconscious bias. I hope that these deeper analyses will address what Martin Luther King, Jr said, "I am sure that none of you would want to rest content with the superficial kind of social analysis that deals merely with effects and does not grapple with underlying causes" (1963).

I will conclude with comments and hopeful ideas from my very *patient* colleagues. And my ending "journey metaphors" will leave us with a visual impression of how I see our current work towards social justice and a higher perspective. Perhaps these views may help us continue to move on and upwards in our efforts to promote a just society and a sound education for all.

I have worked long and hard with my White brothers and sisters to help bring social justice into the forefront and the spotlight in our teacher education programs. From revamping the admissions process to make it more relevant for the diverse and diversity-focused applicant, to initiating programs that would place all of our students for a few weeks or a full year in a culturally or linguistically diverse setting, to personal and professional grappling with the meaning and depth of application of a social justice perspective, we have worked long hours over difficult obstacles with some results.

Still…while I do not doubt the conscious intent of my colleagues, I seriously question their underlying commitment leading to action towards producing authentic long-lasting change. As someone who went to jail in the Free Speech Movement, *womanned* solo pickets for chosen causes and put my professional progress on the line for my beliefs, perhaps I have come to ask for too much. My written works often point to the double standard that seems to exist between people's stated beliefs and their actions. Using excerpts from my writing and my

Louis G. Denti and Patricia A. Whang (eds.), Rattling Chains: Exploring Social Justice in Education, 27–36.
© 2012 Sense Publishers. All rights reserved.

current views, I will be as direct as possible about my painful and increasingly cynical perspective.

I hope that this essay produces the tension we need for growth, as King (1963) said:

> I must confess that I am not afraid of the word 'tension.' I have earnestly opposed violent tension, but there is a type of constructive, nonviolent tension which is necessary for growth. Just as Socrates felt that it was necessary to create a tension in the mind so that individuals could rise from the bondage of myths and half-truths to the unfettered realm of creative analysis and objective appraisal, so must we see the need ... to create the kind of tension in society that will help men rise from the dark depths of prejudice and racism to the majestic heights of understanding and brotherhood.

When we decided to more purposefully pursue a social justice perspective in our program at Oregon State University, we agreed to this statement:

> The purpose of education is to promote a democratic society based on principles of social justice and economic equity. ... We believe that knowledge is a social construction, and that knowledge reflects biases, interests and power that underlie relations between individuals and between groups. A basic task of education is to support students' ability and disposition to analyze experience, as it relates to justice and equity issues, and then to take action to address injustices or problems in that experience. (Moule & Waldschmidt, 2003, p. 122)

As we worked to include a social justice perspective in all aspects of our program it became clear that we did not agree on our approaches to and understanding of social justice. The differences between colleagues – especially those based on race- – as well as our own individual definitions of social justice began to be highlighted as we worked to institute our social justice conceptual framework. Similarly, Zollers, Albert and Cochran-Smith (2000) found this true, and stated that: "Although faculty members unanimously embraced the goal of 'teaching and teacher education for social justice,' they held widely varying ideas about the meaning of social justice" (p. 5). Their study resulted in a continuum for understanding social justice based on the completion of the sentence: "Creating Social Justice requires ...." Answers ranged from "changing individual beliefs" to "taking action collectively." However:

> When the word "racial" is added to "social justice," the stakes are raised and the need for action by groups or individuals of color may be heightened. That is, "... the strategy of those who fight for racial social justice is to unmask and expose racism in all of its various permutations" (Ladson-Billings, 2000, p. 264). Because race is an immutable part of who I am as an African American, the *racial* nature of social justice is an intrinsic experience and automatic expectation for me; I need to do this unmasking. (Moule, 2005, p. 25)

Our different locations on this continuum led to some lively discussions at faculty meetings. As the lone African American faculty member, my comments could threaten both my professional status and carefully forged friendships among my colleagues. Our small faculty with increasing workloads could not find the time for interactional skill building or for discussions about race. It seemed that only when I brought up race and racism that any progress was made in addressing racial issues that often underlie social inequities that need to be justified. An excerpt from a journal article I wrote on this subject, highlights the tension. More specifically:

> While my White colleagues could work toward social justice by acknowledging and challenging socially acceptable notions of racism, such as taking a strong stand against overt racism, I could not. Thomas (2001) found this true in the women she studied. More specifically, "African American women and Latina scholars see a personal mission of *social change* as a fundamental part of their professional responsibilities" (Thomas, 2001, p. 82). My colleagues have not experienced being a person of color in our society and may neither recognize, nor have the same need to fight, more subtle racism. Our differing perceptions and definitions led to dissimilar levels of commitment as well as divergent ways to work towards the goals of our social justice perspective. This lead to the following question:

> The tension between "changing a perspective" versus "taking action" informs the underlying workload issues and ... why our new commitment to social justice had a greater effect on me than on my colleagues. Was there shared responsibility for implementing the faculty's social justice perspective? (Moule, 2005, pp. 25-26)

Later, I add that as:

> our unit began to operationalize the mission statement, we actively recruited part-time faculty and students of color. Photos of students and faculty of color also began appearing on hall displays and on the website. Additionally, we began to include our social justice mission statement as part of the admissions interview, and we became more conscious of the ethnic and gender makeup of the interview teams. The faculty commitment to social justice raised the consciousness of the unit to include social justice advocacy and plans that were not apparent in our prior level of teacher preparation. For example, when we required a social justice component in our work samples, we had to discuss what this meant and add definitions for this in our course syllabi and advising sessions.

> Because I sensed that there would now be stronger support for such work, I began to take independent and individual actions toward implementation of the stated faculty commitment. We all worked hard and some of my colleagues supported my more radical efforts, such as encouraging the entire cohort to live in an inner city for three weeks so that they could student teach in a diverse setting. Nonetheless I ventured into much of this work alone. One obvious reason for my colleagues' reluctance is the everyday pressure of their academic roles. I would suggest an additional factor: the unintentional oversight caused by the ever-present White privilege of not having to factor race into any given equation.

> While we all worked diligently to prepare our students for culturally and linguistically diverse classrooms, for the most part other faculty members' workloads would shift while mine would increase. My actions were more likely to result in extra, not changed work, as I developed new courses and recruited in new ways in new areas of the state. I sensed the need to "reach out of the box" to change things, rather than simply acknowledge the need for change and add on a "color coat" at a superficial level. (Moule, 2005, pp. 29-30)

29

As one committed as I was to social justice my workload increased. Was the work shared? This question prompted me to ask:

> ... the faculty members in our unit to give me specific feedback on their individual efforts to implement our social justice perspective. My email questions included, "Did you recruit students of color for our program outside of the regular channels and process?" and "Did you develop any new courses based on our efforts to implement a social justice perspective?" I also asked a general question about any specific and unique contributions outside of our joint work that they made to implement our social justice perspective. While my colleagues certainly accomplished much in their chosen fields and fulfilled their job descriptions, their answers have helped me to discern that the work I indicated as unique to my role as a faculty member of color in this area of social justice was not shared substantially by others. (Moule, 2005, p. 29)

There was much silence from my colleagues as I asked these questions on commitment and actions. And while I fully understand the workload issues, I believe that this silence may be understood in the context of Martin Luther King Jr.'s (1963) *Letter from Birmingham Jail*. He describes people with this level of commitment as "White moderates." I believe his perspective and analysis could just as easily be called, "liberal academics" because as King (1963) stated:

> I must make two honest confessions to you, my Christian and Jewish brothers. First, I must confess that over the past few years I have been gravely disappointed with the white moderate. I have almost reached the regrettable conclusion that the Negro's great stumbling block in his stride toward freedom is not the White Citizen's Counciler or the Ku Klux Klanner, but the white moderate, who is more devoted to "order" than to justice; who prefers a negative peace which is the absence of tension to a positive peace which is the presence of justice; who constantly says: "I agree with you in the goal you seek, but I cannot agree with your methods of direct action"; who paternalistically believes he can set the timetable for another man's freedom; who lives by a mythical concept of time and who constantly advises the Negro to wait for a "more convenient season." Shallow understanding from people of good will is more frustrating than absolute misunderstanding from people of ill will. Lukewarm acceptance is much more bewildering than outright rejection ....

> Actually, we who engage in nonviolent direct action are not the creators of tension. We merely bring to the surface the hidden tension that is already alive. We bring it out in the open, where it can be seen and dealt with. Like a boil that can never be cured so long as it is covered up but must be opened with all its ugliness to the natural medicines of air and light, injustice must be exposed, with all the tension its exposure creates, to the light of human conscience and the air of national opinion before it can be cured ....

> ... time itself is neutral; it can be used either destructively or constructively. More and more I feel that the people of ill will have used time much more effectively than have the people of good will. We will have to repent in this generation not merely for the hateful words and actions of the bad people but for the appalling silence of the good people ... time itself becomes an ally of the forces of social stagnation. We must use time creatively, in the knowledge that the time is always ripe to do right. Now is the time to make real the promise of democracy and transform our pending national elegy

into a creative psalm of brotherhood. Now is the time to lift our national policy from the quicksand of racial injustice to the solid rock of human dignity.

As a 19 year old I had my own jail experience that set me on a path of painful distrust of many institutions. I learned early to see the superficiality of surface "talk" and described the contexts of those lessons as follows:

It was 1964 and the Free Speech Movement at Berkeley was fomenting. I was a first year student, both idealistic and naïve. I was also a risk taker. Maybe it was my inability to be present in the history making marches in the South at the time. Perhaps I was stirred by the rousing rhetoric of the 1st Amendment. Maybe I was merely seeking a chance to rebel or to express a deeply-felt passion. At any rate, I marched, and I stayed to be arrested. Years later when I became a teacher, this action caused me extra work each licensing period as I explain my arrest. Yet, as a teacher educator, I am glad that I was not afraid to stand up for what I believe is right. But the primary lesson I learned from this experience was a healthy skepticism about the media.

That evening in 1964, Sproul Hall was a risky place to be, especially after the building was locked for the night. My future husband and I were followers, not leaders; yet a series of small events led us to be more noticed than we had planned. We were photographed under a registration table in Sproul Hall, the scene of the action. We were studying. Yet the headline near the photo in the San Francisco Chronicle screamed "Headquarters of the Rebels." I learned then the power of labels not self-chosen. The larger lesson was still to come.

After our arrest, stories came out in newspapers around the nation. I read few, but my interest was piqued when a *New York Times* appeared among our fellow arrestees, for my father lived in New York City. By now we had been released from jail on bail, but I had not decided whether or when to inform my father of my arrest. I wondered what he would make of the story, so I looked over shoulders to get a glimpse. The reader of the newspaper, who I did not know, said, "Who is Jean Golson?" As this is my maiden name, I was suddenly quite interested in reading each detail of this arrest. I also wondered, and I still do, why I, a faceless follower, was chosen out of hundreds to be specifically named by the *Times*. Then, I drank in every detail of the story as told by the *Times* and realized immediately that the story was *not mine*. A journalist had merged a standard arrest and my name. Never again would I fully trust the media, even as I became a correspondent myself. From the age of 19 I have taken everything I read, especially in the media, with a grain of salt, for I knew first hand the falsity in that particular article. This experience was *formative:* "susceptible of transformation by growth and development," because it is clearly part of my transformation and it explains my immunity to certain brands of media hype. (Moule, 2004, p. 165)

From my work as an activist in college, through my tenure at the university and continuing on into my writing and current actions, I see social justice as an *action*, not just an idea to embrace. However, "Not all participants believed that social justice was achievable through the individual construction of new points of view. Some argued that the way to fight for social justice was through activism and political action" (Zoller et al., 2000, p. 9). Similarly:

I believe that social justice means being personally transformed to the point of taking actions to enact or "walk the talk" of one's core beliefs. I believe it means being

> personally transformed and committed to making a difference through critically examining societal issues. This leads to encouraging others to take action whether or not we agree with another's particular course of action or perspective. That is, in a democratic society individuals must work for change even if those actions are opposing. (Moule & Waldschmidt, 2003, p. 127)

We have visited our college's and my own history related to social justice, as well as King's reflections on the nature and timing of our actions. Let us look now at challenging material for the reader's personal consideration, growth and ... will to act.

When I share details of my struggles at my college with an African American colleague in a distant state, he suggested that the silence could be evidence of Helms' (1992) *pseudo-independent stage* among my colleagues, seeking a conscious salving comfort level. Helms explains the overall impact of the stage:

> The Pseudo-Independent stage represents the person's attempt to recapture morality with respect to race. At least in part, he or she does this by "thinking" about racial issues rather than "feeling" about them. Thus, in a psychological sense the person remains aloof from racial issues even though he or she may appear to be actively advocating "liberal" perspectives with respect to such issues .... Pseudo-independent people use a variety of strategies that permit them to maintain their racial comfort .... These strategies also serve the incidental purposes of convincing other Whites that racism has virtually vanished, that people of color who express other convictions are necessarily crazy, irrational, or old fashioned, that if any remnants of racism do exist, they are not the responsibility of the White liberal person to resolve .... Underlying the strategies often is a message to the person of color concerning how he or she should behave in order to allow the White person to continue to feel good about being White .... The Pseudo-Independent stage offers...protective cognitive strategies for not having to worry about emotionally charged issues. (pp. 59-62)

If this is an accurate assessment of my colleagues' stage of racial identity development, then the silence is partially explained by the primary characteristic of the stage, "the capacity to separate intellect from emotions." People with whom I have shared emotional closeness in other ways appear to have little emotional response to my writing and the pain underlying it when we are specifically addressing racial justice. Helms (1992) describes a pseudo-independent stage as signalling the first major movement toward the development of a positive nonracist identity. One of Helms (1992) nine characteristics is key for my understanding: "The person can articulate principles of racial fairness, particularly as long as implementation of such principles have no immediate implications for the person's own life" (p. 59), that is, no action necessary.

In the article *Understanding Unconscious Bias and Unintentional Racism,* I detail a study by Dovidio and Gaertner (2005) that further illuminates the intersection of intent (talk) and action (walk).

> White participants were ... divided into two groups: those who expressed egalitarian views and those who expressed their biases openly. These individuals were then observed to see if their action showed unconscious biases. Each white person then

engaged in a problem-solving task with a black person. The time it took to complete the joint task was recorded.

Table 1. Biased and unbiased white individuals' time to complete paired task.

White Member of Pair	Time to Complete Task with a Black person
Unbiased in word and behavior	4 minutes
Biased in word and behavior	5 minutes
Unbiased by self-report, behavior shows bias	6 minutes

Two important points bear emphasis here. First, the African American individuals, either consciously or unconsciously, were aware of the behavior that showed bias. In this study, "blacks' impressions of whites were related mainly to whites' unconscious attitudes … the uncomfortable and discriminatory behavior associated with aversive racism is very obvious to blacks, even while whites either don't recognize it or consider it hidden" (Dovidio & Gaertner, 2005, pp. 3-4).

Second, white individuals who said they were unbiased, yet showed nonverbal biased behavior, reported their impressions of their behavior related to their *publicly expressed* attitudes and were likely to maintain their stated level of biases when questioned. Therefore, they are likely to blame *the victim*, the black individual, for their slowness in completing the task (and incidentally, possibly reinforce their stereotypes). Sleeter contends, "We cling to filters that screen out what people of color try to tell us because we fear losing material and psychological advantages that we enjoy" (1994, p. 6).

It is important to note that the *well-intentioned* are still racist:

Because aversive racists may not be aware of their unconscious negative attitudes and only discriminate against blacks when they can justify their behavior on the basis of some factor other than race, they will commonly deny any intentional wrongdoing when confronted with evidence of their biases. Indeed, they do not discriminate intentionally. (Dovidio & Gaertner, 2005, p. 5)

I recall sharing with my graduate and undergraduate students that true equity will be reached when 40% of all service positions … meaning hotel housekeepers, groundskeepers, etc., are filled by white men. The loss from 80% of the managerial jobs in this country to 40%, their proportion of the population, would be an actual loss in the number of jobs currently *allotted* to them based on race and gender. That is, they would not have the jobs they may perceive as expected and modeled as their right in the workplace. Can we all embrace such a future? Delpit (1988) maintains, "Liberal educators believe themselves to be operating with good intentions, but these good intentions are only conscious delusions about their unconscious true motives" (p. 285). I am not quite that cynical. I believe in change, slow as it may be. I would add that the only place I have ever seen white male room cleaners in a hotel was at a ski area ... because the job supported a "ski bum" lifestyle.

Over the course of 15 years, I have had interactions with many faculty members. Of those I have worked with, two I would say are close friends. As I put this essay together, I used it as a reason to talk with each privately and candidly. I could list the ways that each has first talked and then walked out some social justice. I could also list ways that I wish they had taken more action. Each shared with me the reasons they have hesitated. Time and fear emerged as did what I consider overarching and key points: Both saw that, no matter how much they might personally take steps both simple – acknowledgement and greetings to those of color, to complex – taking over a difficult teacher education program – they were surrounded by White Hegemony so deep and so embedded that most people were unaware of its existence. One spoke of the tension of being "constantly in the mode of trying to get others to see ... another perspective," yet on walking the talk, she said "it scares me."

The other bittersweet comments I heard from each was how my personal actions and conversations had made a significant impact on their understanding. It is bittersweet because I am so aware of how fraught with peril those moments often were for me. I know that both my colleagues and I had no idea how difficult this journey would be, yet I know our joint struggles made the journey easier.

I would like to conclude this essay with a metaphor that describes my own painful journey and helps put some of our dilemmas around social justice into perspective. More specifically:

> It is as if we are all on a river that flows quietly and gently along. Before I came to this university, I spent most of my time on the banks, dipping in only as necessary. Now, as a faculty member in higher education, I've found myself in this river most of the time. My friends and colleagues float on this river in a strong, sturdy boat of White privilege. The river, our societal mainstream, is simply a given. As is their boat. Although I am a strong swimmer in this mainstream I am in the river more than before and it is increasingly difficult to continue to just wade in and out, swim a while, or float comfortably next to the boat. Every once in a while someone in the boat notices and tosses out an inner tube or holds my hand for a bit. And then some times, someone reaches out and pushes my head under, "Just get over this race thing, Jean." Usually I sputter and resurface and continue on. At a certain point I figure in the long run it makes sense to try to put together a raft for myself. So while continuing to float down the river and engage in conversation and even work through some rapids with those in the boat, I am trying to build this raft with whatever materials I can find. One of the first things that happens is that someone in the boat says, "Hey, how come Jean gets a raft?" If I say, "Because I can't get in the boat with you and I'm getting tired of staying afloat without more support," some say, "What boat?" (Moule, 2012, p. 334)

This metaphor leads us to chilling realizations and uncomfortable tension, the kind that is necessary for growth to the "majestic heights." Many grapple with the complex issues raised by social justice, especially as illustrated in my river metaphor, whether it applies to race or other areas of difference. The challenge for those in the water and for those in the boat is to reach out for each other on our common journey while aiming to make a difference in the very river that carries us all along (adapted from Moule, 2003).

> The travelers stopped to rest. They looked back the way they had come. The path seemed longer and more difficult than they had remembered: Their talk as they walked must have helped to smooth the way. Now that they had the vantage point of the ridge, they saw that what they perceived as a summit had been the beginning of the foothills. They continued on. (Moule, 2012, p. 335)

EXTENSION QUESTIONS/ACTIVITIES

1. In this quote, "Because race is an immutable part of who I am as an African American, the *racial* nature of social justice is an intrinsic experience and automatic expectation for me; I need to do this unmasking" (Moule, 2005, p. 25) she contends that, by the very nature of her race she is put in the position of helping others understand and come to grips with explicit and implicit racial bias and racism. Do you agree or disagree with her contention? Please explain in detail using examples from your personal and professional life.

2. Moule sees social justice as an *action*, not just an idea to embrace. So much ideology surrounds the concept of social justice that putting social justice into action seems like an afterthought. The ideology i.e; we believe strongly in social justice or we treat everyone equally trump putting one's beliefs into action that is clearly identified. At your school/agency do you talk a good social justice game or is social justice noticeable? Think about this last statement and then divide a sheet of paper in half (like a hot dog) and on one side write *Just Social Justice Talk* and on the other side *Social Justice Action – What it Looks Like* and then jot down bullet points under each heading. Share your thoughts in a small group and be ready to share your thoughts with the whole group.

3. As one encounters individuals like Moule in the workplace a tension exists as one comes to a better understanding of oneself through listening closely and understanding a person for whom bias and injustice are common lived experiences. Sometimes individuals who have not experienced discrimination, racial bias or racism dismiss it as too much social justice or (TMSJ) and move away from it, fatigued from the external and internal tension it presents. For the folks on the boat can there be such a thing as too much social justice? For the person in the water can there be such a thing as TMSJ? Use Moule's boat metaphor to critically analyze negative reactions to calls for social justice.

REFERENCES

Delpit, L. D. (1988). The silenced dialogue: Power and pedagogy in educating other people's children. *Harvard Educational Review, 58*(3), 280-299.

Dovidio, J. F., & Gaertner, S. L. (Winter, 2005). Color blind or just plain blind. *The Nonprofit Quarterly, 12*(4).

Helms, J. E. (1992). *A race is a nice thing to have: A guide to being a White person or understanding the White persons in your life.* New York: Greenwood.

King, M. L., Jr. (1963). *A letter from Birmingham jail.*

Moule, J. (2003, June). *Aiming to make a difference.* Commencement Address at Oregon State University, Corvallis.

Moule, J. (2004). Safe and growing out of the box. In J. J. Romo, P. Bradfield, & R. Serrano (Eds.), *Reclaiming democracy: Multicultural educators' journeys toward transformative teaching* (pp. 147-171). Upper Saddle River, NJ: Merrill Prentice Hall.

Moule, J. (2005). Implementing a social justice perspective in teacher education: Invisible burden for faculty of color. *Teachers and Teacher Education Research, 32*(4), 23-42.

Moule, J. (2009). Understanding unconscious bias and unintentional racism. *Phi Delta Kappan, 90*(5), 320-326.

Moule, J. (2012). *Cultural competence: A primer for educators,* 2nd ed. Belmont, CA: Cengage.

Moule, J., & Waldschmidt, E. D. (2003). Face to face over race: Personal challenges from instituting a social justice perspective in our teacher education program. *Teacher Education and Practice, 16*(2), 121-142.

Zollers, N. J., Albert, L. R., & Cochran-Smith, M. (2000). In pursuit of social justice. Collaborative research and practice in teacher education. *Action in Teacher Education, 22*(2), 1-14.

Jean Moule
Emerita, Oregon State University

NEL NODDINGS

WORKING TO AWAKEN: SOCIAL JUSTICE AND VOCATIONAL EDUCATION

"Social justice" has become a contentious term. To most of us it means non-discrimination on the basis of race, gender, ethnicity, religion, or sexual orientation. But to many of us it also means the elimination of gross poverty and the practices that support it. It is the emphasis on the elimination of poverty that leads some critics to equate social justice with socialism. They want no part of government programs to redistribute the wealth.

In schools, concern for social justice has led thoughtful educators to recommend that tracking be abandoned. They argue that it is not *just* to give privileged youngsters strong courses that prepare them for college and well-paying jobs while their less privileged peers are assigned to dead-end courses that condemn them to ill-paying jobs or unemployment. To be just, they assert, we must provide equal educational opportunities to all of our students.

Although I have great sympathy for my colleagues who oppose tracking, I will argue here that we have made a serious mistake by equating "equal" with "same" in revising the secondary school curriculum. In accordance with this thinking, many school districts now require all students to take college preparatory courses regardless of their interests or abilities. Failure rates are high, the graduation rates are low, the need for remedial courses in college has remained high or increased, and the quality of many high school courses has deteriorated. As educators, we are on the wrong track.

There are two distinct but related senses of the word *tracking*. In one, students are assigned (or tracked) to a class on the basis of their ability in the subject to be taught. Reading groups in elementary school are an example of such tracking, and ability groupings in mathematics appear at every level. In this brief essay, I will not discuss this form of tracking. In the second form, the one that interests me here, we provide different *tracks* or *programs* for secondary school students with different interests and/or capabilities. The basic idea seems entirely compatible with social justice in a liberal democracy. Students should be given a choice among equally rich, well-designed programs relevant to their interests. Notice that I emphasize *choice* here; students should not be arbitrarily assigned to a track. Their choice should be carefully guided, and it should be possible to switch tracks if the initial choice does not work out.

It does not seem to be "socially just" to force all students into a program designed to satisfy the talents and interests of a few. It has been argued that, in the

Louis G. Denti and Patricia A. Whang (eds.), Rattling Chains: Exploring Social Justice in Education, 37–40.
© 2012 *Sense Publishers. All rights reserved.*

name of economic justice, all students should be given the opportunity to prepare for college. I agree enthusiastically that they should have this opportunity if they request it. However, it can hardly be called an "opportunity" if students are forced into it. In justifying a universal college-for-all curriculum, some even insist that a college education is required in order to obtain a decent job and be part of the middle-class. Is this true? And if it is, should it be so in a socially just society? Should we tell our kids, in essence, go to college or be nothing?

It is understandable that educators concerned with social justice have reacted angrily against tracking as it has been practiced throughout most of the twentieth century. The tracks were valued and organized hierarchically with the college preparatory track at the top and the vocational at the bottom, and students were often assigned to tracks on the basis of race or socio-economic status, not by interest or ability. To make matters worse, courses in the "lower" tracks were often poorly designed and badly taught. In a school where I taught for a while, one teacher regularly addressed his lower track kids as "you punks." The practice was deplorable and clearly incompatible with social justice.

But there is an alternative to the elimination of tracking. If we are seriously committed to social justice, we could design excellent programs in vocational education. In much of Western Europe, school people, unions, and employers design such programs cooperatively, and attention is given not only to vocational preparation but also to personal and civic development (Hoffman 2010). These programs are meant to be educational programs, not simply training programs. Broad cooperation ensures that graduates will have a good chance to obtain jobs that pay reasonably well. We could get valuable ideas from a study of these programs, but we need not copy them exactly. In particular, we may want to put greater emphasis on choice than other countries do, and our commercial/industrial needs may well be somewhat different.

In the democratic society envisioned by John Dewey and Walt Whitman, citizens were to work together, recognize their interdependence, communicate effectively, solve problems collaboratively, and respect the contributions of all workers. Common sense tells us that we need one another. Social justice demands that we respect one another's work. No person who works at a fulltime, honest job should live in poverty. Nor should we suppose that those who work with their hands are somehow lacking in intellect.

In the past few years, several writers have described the intellectual possibilities in many forms of hands-on work. Crawford (2009) has given us a picture of the complexities and beauties of motorcycle repair, and Rose (2005) has vividly described the "mind at work." Recently, Rose (1995) has expressed concern that his work might be used to justify the practice of tracking. If the practice were to continue with all the intellectual and ethical faults it exhibited in the twentieth century, I too would be concerned about it. But we do not overcome one form of social injustice by replacing it with another.

Thoughtful opponents of tracking should also consider why the practice of forcing all kids into college preparatory courses has been so widely accepted – even by many people who are wary of a commitment to social justice. Might it be that it is cheaper to put all kids into "standard" algebra classes than to create and maintain a variety of programs? Good vocational education is *much* more expensive than standard academic education. Further, if all students have the opportunity to prepare for college, we can claim that it is their own fault if they don't "make it" and wind up by default in low-paying jobs. We can insist that we have acted in good faith by offering equal opportunity.

If we are committed to social justice, we should make a concerted effort to eliminate poverty. This is primarily a *social* problem, not an educational problem. As educators, we should provide a variety of programs in our schools, any one of which a student can be proud to join (Noddings, 2007).

In conclusion, I want to make it clear that, when I argue against college for all, I am not arguing against all forms of post-secondary education. On the contrary, I believe that most people can profit from postsecondary study. But note that post-secondary education requires the completion of secondary education, and we lose far too many students in our high schools. Perhaps we should curb our enthusiasm for preparing all kids for college and concentrate on getting more of them through high school.

As a society, we are at a juncture very like the one faced by educators and policymakers at the start of the twentieth century. There were heated arguments then over plans to extend high school education to all students. Those arguing in favor of the extension pointed to the nation's transition from an agricultural to an industrial base, one that required more education. They argued also that the enormous flood of new immigrants required further education to ensure a well-informed, proud, and loyal citizenry. They were right.

Those opposed argued that many children, perhaps most, could not succeed with the classical curriculum that characterized the secondary academies of the time. They too were right.

The ingenious answer was to change the concept of secondary education, and the comprehensive high school was born. Even today there are people who think that was a mistake. But look at the record! In 1900, only about 7% of our population graduated from high school. By 1970, more than 75% did so. It was a remarkable achievement, and it made American education a model for the world.

Now we are arguing over whether all students should go to college. Those who advocate this move point to the change from an industrial to a technical/information society. They are right that something has to change. Those opposed argue that not all students can profit from a traditional college education, and we are cheating students who need a different sort of education. They too are right. We should change our conception of post-secondary education. Doing that requires a dramatic change in secondary education. Preparation for traditional college work is not appropriate for all forms of post-secondary education. This contention, of course, requires further argument, and we should launch the debate. If my argument holds up, we should put our minds to work on designing and implementing new programs that meet the requirements of social justice.

EXTENSION QUESTIONS/ACTIVITIES

1. We have moved from a manufacturing society to an informational society and in order to compete in the new society many, if not most, believe that a college degree is a necessity. Noddings turns that notion on its head. Make a strong argument for or against the notion that everyone needs a college degree to be part of the new society.

2. Do you think vocational education proposed by Noddings is antithetical to a construct of social justice that strives for fairness and equitable opportunity for all? Answer this question starting with your definition of social justice and then establish a propositional argument for or against vocational education nowadays.

3. If you had it your way, what should a high school curriculum include? If vocational education is part of your curriculum explain how it would manifest itself i.e., as a separate academy, a series of courses. Would a student earn a diploma or a certificate of completion? Explain your answers in detail and be prepared to share with a colleague or in a small group.

REFERENCES

Crawford, M.B. (2009). *Shop class as soulcraft.* New York: Penguin Press.

Hoffman, N. (2010). Learning for jobs, not 'college for all': How European countries think about preparing young people for productive citizenship. *Teachers College Record*, retrieved August 3, 2011, from http://www.tcrecord.org ID Number: 16096.

Rose, M. (1995). *Possible Lives: The promise of public education in America* Boston: Houghton Mifflin.

Rose, M. (2005). *The mind at work: Valuing the intelligence of the American worker.* New York: Penguin.

Noddings, N. (2007). *When school reform goes wrong.* New York: Teachers College Press.

Nel Noddings
Stanford University

CURT DUDLEY-MARLING

WORKING TO AWAKEN: DOES "DOING GOOD" EQUAL SOCIAL JUSTICE?

Boston College is a Jesuit university where there is a strong emphasis on the theme of social justice. Social justice appears in course titles, program descriptions, and departmental and university mission statements. The school of Arts and Sciences offers an interdisciplinary minor in "Faith, Peace, and Justice" and the university points with pride to its students' involvement in a range of service activities as an instantiation of the institution's commitment to social justice. The Teacher Education department in which I work has made social justice one of five themes that underpin our teacher preparation program. These themes appear on all of our course syllabi. The theme "Promoting Social Justice" is described as follows: "We see teaching as an activity with political dimensions, and we see all educators as responsible for challenging inequities in the social order and working with others to establish a more just society." My department routinely surveys the graduates of our program to assess the effectiveness our teacher preparation program and many of the questions we ask them relate to social justice. Social justice is also the core theme of our doctoral program to which we have attracted many bright and socially committed doctoral students.

Still, faculty and students in our department struggle over the meaning of social justice. Some faculty equate social justice with the fair treatment of individual students, even the children of privilege who fill the classrooms at Boston College. Others associate social justice with working with vulnerable or at-risk populations. For these folks, working in urban schools or in special education classrooms evidences our commitment to social justice. Other faculty and students – and I include myself in this latter group – take a more systemic view of social justice, focusing on the role of schooling in ameliorating the inequitable distribution of social and economic goods in our society. This includes addressing the so-called achievement gap by providing all students with the kind of rich, engaging curricular experiences found in schools attended by the most privileged in our society. Ultimately, we believe that teaching for social justice is a "means by which educators work to expose and dismantle individual, cultural, and institutional oppression through critical consciousness raising and critical multicultural pedagogy wherein students are taught to challenge information and work for social change in the classroom" (Hyland & Heuschkel, 2010, p. 822).

Differences over the meaning of social justice in our department reflect broader debates over the meaning of social justice in the media and society. For some, social justice is associated with a sinister, left-wing political agenda. In his now

Louis G. Denti and Patricia A. Whang (eds.), Rattling Chains: Exploring Social Justice in Education, 41–46.
© 2012 *Sense Publishers. All rights reserved.*

infamous rant about social justice, TV personality Glenn Beck urged his listeners to "look for the words 'social justice' or 'economic justice' on your church Web site. If you find it, run as fast as you can" (Goodstein, 2010). Writing on the Fox News website, Beck defined "social justice" as the "forced redistribution of wealth with a hostility toward individual property rights, under the guise of charity and/or justice" (Glenn Beck, 2010).

Critics of teacher education associate the social justice mission of many schools of education with a liberal political ideology aimed at promoting multiculturalism, socialism, feminism, gay rights – and just making children "feel good" – over teaching critical skills like reading, writing, and math (Cochran-Smith, Barnatt, Lahann, Shakman, & Terrell, 2009). Those critical of the social justice agenda of teacher education also complain that the ideology underpinning social justice has the effect of silencing or excluding from teaching those who do not share the values associated with social justice (Cochran-Smith et al., 2009).

Of course, liberal schools of education are not the only places where a commitment to social justice can be found. As Glenn Beck discovered, there was a furious backlash to his commentary on social justice from many mainline churches (including the Church of Latter Day Saints of which Beck is a member) that embrace social justice as a value that is central to their religious mission. Often this translates into work on behalf of the poor and disadvantaged but may include efforts to affect the conditions that give rise to poverty and discrimination (Goodstein, 2010). Still, the social justice stance of many "mainline" churches does not extend to gays and lesbians or even women.

Advocates of free market ideology also use the language of social justice to promote their goals for a society organized around the principle that the well being of individuals can best be advanced "by liberating individual entrepreneurial freedoms and skills within an institutional framework characterized by strong private property rights, free markets, and free trade" (Harvey, 2005, p. 2). A free-market version of social justice "merely requires that individuals be given access to markets. If they fail to achieve educational and economic success, then individuals only have themselves to blame" (Hursh, 2009, p. 162). From this perspective, disproportionate levels of failure among poor, Black, and Hispanic students, for example, demonstrates personal failures and a lack of entrepreneurial virtues or ability (Harvey, 2005; Murray, 2009), not a problem of social justice.

Even this brief review makes it clear that social justice is a contested term used differently by different stakeholders in different contexts (Hyland & Heuschkel, 2010). Ultimately, the meaning of social justice turns on your conception of the ideal society (Hursh, 2009). Below I examine the meaning of social justice in the context of educating students with disabilities. I begin by considering whether the practice of special education ("doing good") is, as some of our colleagues would argue – almost by definition – an instantiation of social justice. I argue that, despite the worthy intentions of special educators, special education, as an institution, sustains a status quo in schools that is fundamentally unjust. Finally, I consider what a socially just alternative to traditional special education might look like.

IS SPECIAL EDUCATION SOCIALLY JUST?

Ayers, Quinn, and Stovall (2009) identify equity as one of the three pillars of social justice education. They define equity in education as

> The principle of fairness, equal access to the most challenging and nourishing educational experiences, the demand that what the most privileged and enlightened are able to provide their children must be the standard for what is made available to all children. (p. xiv)

Cochran-Smith et al. (2009) offer a similar perspective on social justice in schools arguing that "from the perspective of social justice, promoting pupils' learning includes teaching much of the traditional canon, but it also includes teaching pupils to think critically about and challenge the universality of that knowledge" (p. 635).

But many students in our schools do not experience curricula that are challenging, nourishing, or critical. Many students with disabilities and other children who struggle in school – including disproportionate numbers of children living in poverty, Black and Hispanic students, and English language learners – experience a circumscribed curricula that emphasize low level *skills* in contrast to the rich, challenging curriculum typically experienced by the most successful students, a group that includes disproportionate numbers of affluent, white students. Certainly there are examples of students with disabilities being challenged with the sort of rich curriculum common in upper academic tracks. The OLE project (Ruiz, Vargas, & Beltrán, 2002), for example, brings to bilingual, special education classrooms the kind of rich, challenging curricula common in programs for gifted students. Many literacy educators have also advocated literature rich, meaning-based reading and writing curricula for students with disabilities (Allington, 2005; Dudley-Marling & Paugh, 2004; Kliewer, 2008; Rhodes & Dudley-Marling, 1988). However, special education is dominated by a deficit approach that situates learning failure in the minds, bodies, language, and culture of students who struggle in school and aims to "fix" students and their families by focusing on lower-level (basic) skills.

To the degree that poor and minority students are overrepresented in special education (Harry & Klingner, 2006), the structures of special education participate in the re-segregation of American schools (Kozol, 2006) and the maintenance of a status quo in which the rich getter richer (through challenging curriculum) and the poor, disadvantaged, and disabled get basic skills instruction that severely limits their educational and vocational opportunities. Gabel and Connor (2009) conclude that the institutional practice of special education "is implicated in resegregating schools ... watering down curriculum ... stigmatizing difference" (p. 377) and the dehumanizing of people with differences. The overwhelming majority of special educators are good, caring people motivated by the best intentions. Yet, the practice of special education often "supports, rather than challenges, dominant hegemony, prevailing social hierarchies, and inequitable distributions of power and privilege" (Gorski, 2008, p. 515).

A SOCIALLY JUST APPROACH TO EDUCATION FOR
STUDENTS WITH DISABILITIES

A socially just approach to educating students with disabilities begins with the rejection of deficit thinking that pathologizes students with disabilities as people in need of "fixing." An alternative, social constructivist framework, presumes that all students are smart, competent people (Biklen, 2005; Miller, 1993) entitled to the sort of rich curricular opportunities experienced by the most successful students as opposed to the fragmented, low level skills approach that emerges from a deficit perspective (Dudley-Marling & Paugh, 2005). In this (social constructivist) formulation, disabilities are a "cultural fabrication" (McDermott & Varenne, 1995) created in the context of human relations and institutions. As they put it, "One cannot be disabled alone" (p. 337). Gergen (1990) puts it this way:

> By and large we may view the common practice of holding single individuals responsible for achievements or deficits in human understanding as an exercise in practicalrhetoric ... it is also problematic to discredit failing students ... for their failure in understanding. ... Such individuals are constituents of a complex array of relationships, and it is inappropriate from the present standpoint to disembed their actions from the relational sequences of which they are a part. (p. 587)

A social constructivist perspective implicates institutional structures and the conditions of schooling in the construction of disabilities. Normative assessment practices designed to produce failure, rigid, age-graded curricula, one-size-fits all instructional programs, and differential curricular practices that limit the academic and vocational possibilities of many students all participate in the construction (or "fabrication") of disabilities.

A deficit orientation begins with the question: What's wrong with this student? Alternatively, a social constructivist perspective asks: how do we create inclusive schools and classrooms organized to produce success, not failure? What do schools that accept human differences as *normal* and not as evidence of pathology look like? How do we structure schools that enable teachers to provide individual support and direction that responds to the needs of individual students and treat differences in language, culture, and experience as assets?

Research-based methods and Response-to-Intervention (RTI) that focuses on the amelioration of student deficiencies are inadequate to the task of creating inclusive schools and classrooms. Creating truly inclusive schools requires the transformation of the structures of schooling that produce so much failure in the first place. Reading and writing workshops, inquiry circles (Harvey & Daniels, 2009), and cooperative grouping (Cohen, 1994), for example, have the potential to accommodate the range of differences students bring with them to school, but these practices will always be limited in the context of the regimen of high stakes testing and accountability that has dominated educational reform the last decade. Creating inclusive, socially just schools requires a radical transformation of schooling that begins with the question, "what do socially just schools like?" And the answer to this question must include the voices of those who have been excluded, including students with disabilities. If students don't experience schooling as inclusive then it is neither inclusive nor socially just. It is likely that one of the primary reasons so many students experience schooling as oppressive is that educators and educational policy makers rarely listen to the voices of the oppressed.

EXTENSION QUESTIONS/ACTIVITIES

1. Curt Dudley-Marling provides two meanings of social justice that divide the faculty in his department. With which position do you find most agreement, those who place an emphasis on "fair treatment of individual students" or emphasize "working with vulnerable or at-risk populations?

2. The author describes different responses to student failure, in broad terms, as those that blame the education system versus those that blame the student. How might each of these focuses influence the practice of instruction?

3. Describe what you believe to be two "good" educational practices and how do they fit in the author's schema of social justice.

4. In your view what should a school that advocates and promotes social justice look like? Articulate your thoughts first on paper and then in small cooperative groups share your perceptions.

REFERENCES

Allington, R. L. (2005). What really matters for struggling readers: Designing research-based programs (2nd edition). Boston, MA: Allyn & Bacon.

Ayers, W., Quinn, T., & Stovall, D. (Eds.). (2009). *Handbook of social justice in education*. New York: Routledge.

Beck, G. (2010). "What is social justice?" Foxnews.com. http://www.foxnews.com/story/0,2933,589832,00.html, retrieved October 5, 2010.

Biklen, D. (2005). *Autism and the myth of the person alone*. New York: University Press.

Cochran-Smith, M., Barnatt, J., Lahann, R., Shakman, K., & Terrell, D. (2009). Teacher education for social justice: Critiquing the critics. In W. Ayers, T. Quinn, & D. Stovall (Eds.), *Handbook of social justice in education* (pp. 625-639). New York: Routledge.

Cohen, E. (1994). *Designing group work: Strategies for the heterogeneous classroom*. New York: Teachers College Press.

Dudley-Marling, C. & Paugh, P. (2005). The rich get richer, the poor get Direct Instruction. In B. Altwerger (Ed.), *Reading for profit: How the bottom line leaves kids behind* (pp. 156-171). Portsmouth, NH: Heinemann.

Dudley-Marling, C., & Paugh, P. (2004). *A classroom teacher's guide to struggling readers*. Portsmouth, NH: Heinemann.

Dudley-Marling, C., & Paugh, P. (2009). *A classroom teacher's guide to struggling writers*. Portsmouth, NH: Heinemann.

Gabel, S. L., & Connor, D. J. (2009). Theorizing disability: Implications and applications for social justice in education. In W. Ayers, T. Quinn, & D. Stovall (Eds.), *Handbook of social justice in education* (pp. 377-399). New York: Routledge.

Gergen, K. J. (1990). Social understanding and the inscription of self. In J. W. Sigler, R. A. Shweder, & G. Herdt (Eds.), *Cultural psychology: Essays on comparative human development* (pp. 569-606). New York: Cambridge University Press.

Goodstein, L. (March 12, 2010) Outraged by Glenn Beck's salvo, Christians fire back. *New York Times*, A12.

Gorski, P. (2008). Good intentions are not enough: A colonizing intercultural education. *Intercultural Education, 19*, 515-525.

Harry, B., & Klingner, J. (2006). *Why are there so many minority children in special education?* New York: Teachers College Press.

Harvey, D. (2005). *A brief history of neoliberalism*. New York: Oxford University Press.

Harvey, S., & Daniels, H. (2009). *Comprehension and collaboration: Inquiry circles in action*. Portsmouth, NH: Heinemann.

Hursh, D. (2009). Beyond the justice of the market: Combating neoliberal educational discourse and promoting deliberative democracy and economic equality. In W. Ayers, T. Quinn, & D. Stovall, (Eds.), *Handbook of social justice in education* (pp. 152-164). New York: Routledge.

Hyland, N.E. & Neuschkel, K., (2010). Fostering understanding of institutional oppression among U.S. pre-service teachers. *Teaching and Teacher Education: An International Journal of Research and Studies, 26*(4), 821-829.

Kliewer, C. (2008). *Seeing all kids as readers: A new version for literacy in the inclusive early childhood classroom*. Baltimore, MD: Paul Brookes.

Kozol, J. (2006). *The shame of the nation: The restoration of apartheid schooling in America*. New York: Three Rivers Press.

McDermott, R., & Varenne, H. (1995). Culture as disability. *Anthropology and Education Quarterly, 26*, 323-348.

Miller, L. (1993). *What we call smart: A new narrative for intelligence and learning*. San Diego: Singular.

Murray, C. (2009). *Real education. Four simple truths for bringing America's schools back to reality*. New York: Three Rivers Press.

Rhodes, L.K., & Dudley-Marling, C. (1988). *Readers and writers with a difference: A holistic approach to teaching literacy to LD and remedial students*. Portsmouth, NH: Heinemann Educational Books.

Ruiz, N., Vargas, E., & Beltrán, A. (2002). Becoming a reader and writer in a bilingual special education classroom. *Language Arts, 79*, 297-309.

Curt Dudley-Marling
Boston University

PATRICIA A. WHANG

SECTION 2: INTRODUCTION

The Personal Is Political

The touchstone for the essays in this section revolves around the idea that social justice is an action that is both initiated and sustained by a sense of empathy and compassion for others and the suffering they are experiencing. This makes sense because if one neither feels a sense of connection nor cares about another's trials and tribulations, then what will spur him/her out of complacency to take action? Or as Cammorata (this volume) explains in an earlier essay: "Showing empathy for people who suffer from pressures impalpable in one's personal context builds a sense of compassion that aspires to bettering the world for all" (p. 10). Compassion is understood to arise with prolonged contact with the physical, material, and/or psychological suffering of others (Hanh, 2001). Compassionate acts require being mindful of suffering and doing everything in our power to ease that suffering. Compassion is not a feeling of pity, superiority, or judgment. It is a feeling of togetherness, based on the understanding that whatever happens to one affects us all.

Unfortunately, one is unlikely to develop empathy or compassion towards those who remain little more than embodiments of stereotypes or members of groups that are consistently portrayed negatively in the media. Like most societies, we live in a socially segmented society, that reflects people's choices about "whom to befriend, whom to marry, where to live, to which schools to send their children, and so on. Factors like race, ethnicity, social class and religious affiliation influence these associational choices" (Loury, n.d., sec. 2. Social segmentation and Economic Inequality, para. 3). Therefore, personal experiences are unlikely to challenge our preconceptions of others. Kennedy (1987) is worth quoting at length because he offers concrete examples that push us toward a deeper understanding and he also offers connections to points made in Section 1: Introduction. As Kennedy (1987) explains:

> To the non-poor the poor are all but invisible. The non-poor live in such isolation from the poor that they easily hide in their cocoon and blame the victims because they neither know their hurts nor understand the causes of such hardships as layoffs and unemployment .... Just as superhighways hide the realities of urban poverty from commuters driving by, so does the cocoon of ideology mask the realities of the world beyond the comfortable social location of the non-poor .... What the cocoon does is cushion the problems and make the suffering seem remote. It narrows the ideological

Louis G. Denti and Patricia A. Whang (eds.), Rattling Chains: Exploring Social Justice in Education, 47–50.
© 2012 *Sense Publishers. All rights reserved.*

horizons, circumscribes interpretations, and severely limits imaginations which could envision a better world. (p. 240)

As a countervailing force, it is necessary to cross boundaries and bridge distances. Intentionally crossing boundaries and bridging distances is necessary because it is too easy to maintain what Martin (1999) refers to as "aerial distance." This phrase refers to the maintenance of such great distance from the lived experiences of others – especially those who are negotiating life from dominated social positions – that we remain unaware or have little first hand knowledge of their joys, triumphs, pain, suffering and horror. Knowledge derived from distanced perspectives is necessarily diluted, possibly distorted, and most problematically possibly non-existent. hooks (1993) has likewise written about the importance of being able to empathize, or feel with and for experiences that are not our own, especially if we are to build community with those whom we might not naturally do so. Furthermore, such distance dilutes any sense of agency, decreases the likelihood of alliances being forged, and suppresses moral imagination. Maxine Greene (1995) has been eloquent in her refusal to abandon a moral imagination that would awaken and free people to realize that things could be otherwise – better than they are. Without such an imagination it may be difficult to ignite the will to act with compassion.

The chapters in this section illuminate the power and potency inherent in sharing and analyzing stories, not just because bringing to voice personal experiences may be therapeutic for the story-teller ("The Personal Is Political: The original feminist theory paper at the author's web site," n.d.), but because of the ways how stories can raise awareness, bridge distance, and create community. More specifically, stories may begin the process of personally confronting the listener with a reality that demands a response. Evans (1987) has described this process as the root of a transformative educational experience. Developing empathy requires "truth telling," or opportunities for communities to be able to know the truth, as well as speak openly and honestly (hooks, 1993). Furthermore, hooks (1994) elaborates on the importance of truth telling in *Teaching to Transgress* when she upholds the importance of "hearing each other's voices, individual thoughts, and sometimes associating these voices with personal experience" (p. 186). Truth telling allows us to become more acutely aware of each other. This greater awareness is important, because empathy or compassion requires recognizing the suffering of others. As The Dalai Lama (2001) explains, developing empathy, or a sense of closeness to others that is expressed through feelings of responsibility or of concern, requires being able to look at the world from a less self-centered perspective. Stories provide opportunities to look at the world from vantage points other than one's own.

For this second section, the phrase "Cultivating Compassion" is included in the titles that constitute for the essays in this section as a reminder of emergent insights. More specifically, this section begins with *Riane Eisler's* description of the events that stoked her moral imagination, as a child, to re-vision a truly caring society. She then affords us an opportunity to examine how her professional life has coalesced around efforts to make good on that vision. Simultaneously, we are reminded of the importance of culture, especially as brokered by societal institutions such as family, in shaping the perspectives, practices, policies, and values that members of that society must negotiate from their societal positioning – which in Eisler's case had to do with her family's religious/ethnic background and economic status. Then, *Robert Rueda's* essay presents us with a different vantage point, that of a researcher working in classrooms that serve children who are socially positioned on the periphery because of the languages they do or do not speak. His stories are potent reminders that, especially as educators, our commitments, beliefs, and actions impact how students understand the world and their place in it. Some of the threads traced in Eisler and Rueda's essays continue in *Ronald David Glass'* brutally honest re-telling of events that spanned his childhood, adolescence, and first teaching experiences. His stories make it hard to ignore the lack of caring that can be experienced, as well as the differences that caring and intentionally struggling to achieve and maintain equitable treatment and opportunities for all can make. Building concretely on a point made by Eisler, regarding the importance of probing the interrelationship between the private sphere of the family and the public sphere of the state, Glass provides a clear example of how family can not only provide necessary tools and dispositions, but also serve as co-conspirators and/or role models to counteract an unjust public sphere. Similarly, *Mara Sapon-Shevin* has chosen to take us into the private sphere and use parenting stories to provoke our moral imagination about what wide-awake caring looks like and how it can be nurtured. Finally, using vignettes, *Brown* brings to our awareness, a consideration of how, as a society, we have chosen to respond to the needs of fellow citizens with significant intellectual disabilities. Examining the past treatment of a group that cannot advocate for themselves makes it apparent that such silence can mute compassionate societal responses. Recent gains in achievement for this group, however, highlight the importance of committing to social justice for all. In this section, the essays remind us that interest in social justice is not an abstract academic exercise. Rather, the conclusions that one draws and the commitments that one does or does not honor have very real implications for the lives of living, breathing, and striving people.

REFERENCES

Evans, R. A. (1987). Education for emancipation: Movement toward transformation. In *Pedagogies for the non-poor* (pp. 257-284). Maryknoll, NY: Orbis Books.

Greene, M. (1995). Art and imagination. *Phi Delta Kappan, 76*, 378-383.

Hanh, T. N. (2001). Embracing anger. *Plum village.* http://www.plumvillage.org/. Retrieved December 5, 2002, from www.plumvillage.org/TNH/embracing_anger.htm.

hooks, b. (1993). A life in the spirit: Reflections on faith and politics. *ReVision, 15*, 99-105.

hooks, bell. (1994). *Teaching to transgress: Education as the practice of freedom.* Routledge.

Kennedy, W. B. (1987). The ideological captivity of the non-poor. In *Pedagogies for the non-poor* (pp. 232-256). Maryknoll, NY: Orbis Books.

Lama, T. D. (2001). *Ethics for the new millennium.* Riverhead Trade.

Loury, G. C. (n.d.). The divided society and the democratic idea. Retrieved March 30, 2012, from http://www.bu.edu/irsd/articles/divided.htm.

Martin, J. R. (1999). *Coming of age in academe: Rekindling women's hopes and reforming the academy* (1st ed.). Routledge.

The Personal Is Political: The original feminist theory paper at the author's web site. (n.d.). Retrieved September 3, 2011, from http://www.carolhanisch.org/CHwritings/PIP.html.

RIANE EISLER

CULTIVATING COMPASSION: LESSONS LEARNED FROM SOCIETY AND CULTURE

For me, social justice is not, and never has been, an abstraction.

I experienced injustice very early in my life, when my father was arrested simply because he happened to be Jewish. On Crystal Night, so called because of all the glass shattered in Jewish homes, businesses, and synagogues that night a gang of Gestapo men broke into our home. My father tried to hide, but they found him, and as happened to many men during this night of Nazi terrorism against Jews, they beat him, pushed him down the stairs, and dragged him off. So when I was still a very little girl, I saw insensitivity, cruelty, and violence.

But I also witnessed something else that fateful night: our impulse to stand up against injustice and our great capacity for love. My mother recognized one of the Gestapo men as a former errand boy for the family business. Angrily, she confronted him for betraying a man who had been good to him. My mother could have been killed, as many people were that night. But by a miracle she was not, and eventually she obtained my father's release.

Shortly afterwards we escaped from Vienna, thus avoiding the fate met by most of my family – aunts, uncles, cousins, grandparents – who were murdered in Nazi concentration camps. We fled to Cuba and I grew up in the industrial slums of Havana, where I witnessed yet another form of injustice: the enormous gaps between haves and have not's that at the time condemned most Cubans to abject poverty.

In my child's mind it was clear that these injustices were wrong. Eventually it also became clear that I had to work for a world where people are not hated and persecuted just because they are of a different religion or ethnic background, and where a few do not have great riches while others starve: a world where people actually care for one another rather than just talk about justice and compassion.

Indeed, in addressing the question of what is social justice I want to start with this matter of caring. Because ultimately empathy and caring, or their absence, lie at the core of how we treat one another.

WHAT IS JUSTICE AND WHAT IS SOCIAL?

Justice has been defined in many different ways. Some are barbaric, as when Stalin and PotPol murdered millions in the name of building a more just society, or when women in Muslim fundamentalist cultures are, in the name of a just morality,

Louis G. Denti and Patricia A. Whang (eds.), Rattling Chains: Exploring Social Justice in Education, 51–57.
© 2012 *Sense Publishers. All rights reserved.*

slowly stoned to death for any suspected sexual independence. So without empathy, without caring, justice can mean terrible things.

Social, that is, how we label a society, is also defined in many different ways. We've been taught to classify societies in terms of right vs. left, religious vs. secular, capitalist vs. socialist, Eastern vs. Western, Northern vs. Southern, or industrial vs. pre or post industrial. These labels are useful in identifying a society's ideological or economic orientation, geographic location, or level of technological development.

But these old categories do not help answer the most fundamental question for our future. This question, fundamental to social justice, lies behind my multidisciplinary, cross-cultural research: What kinds of conditions support our human capacities for sensitivity, caring, and creativity, or, alternately, for insensitivity, cruelty, and destructiveness?

I brought a wide-ranging background to this research. After obtaining a degree in sociology, my first job was at an offshoot of the Rand Corporation at a time when systems analysis, the study of how different parts of a system interact to determine its character, was just getting off the ground. Some years later, I obtained a law degree at UCLA, which I used to work in the civil rights movement and then for women's rights.

I founded the Los Angeles Women's Center Legal program, the first in the country. I wrote a Friend of the Court brief to the U.S. Supreme Court proposing the then radical idea that women should be considered persons under the Equal Protection Clause of the 14th Amendment. I testified at government hearings, drafted legislation, wrote a book about the new no-fault divorce laws that predicted what later became known as the "feminization of poverty," and wrote the only mass paperback on the proposed Equal Rights Amendment to the U.S. Constitution (Eisler, 1978).

When that amendment, which merely said the "Equality of rights under the law shall not be denied or abridged by the United States or any State on the basis of sex," was defeated, I predicted this would signal a period of regression, as it marked the first time an expansion of constitutional protection had been blocked. And so it was: the Rightist-Fundamentalist alliance that today holds us hostage to a "morality" of fear, insensitivity, and exclusion, first came together to defeat the ERA, a matter that many people who consider themselves progressive still think of as "just a women's issue."

So when I embarked on my study of society, I brought a perspective that, unlike most studies (still aptly called "the study of man") takes into account the *whole* of society: both its female and male halves. This made it possible to understand why pushing women back to their "traditional" or subordinate place is a priority for people who believe humanity is composed of "superiors" ordained by God or nature to dominate and "inferiors" ordained to be dominated. It also made it possible to see social configurations that are invisible from the perspective of conventional social categories (Eisler, 1998, 2008).

SOCIAL JUSTICE AND THE PRIMARY HUMAN RELATIONS

A core principle of systems analysis is that understanding and changing a system requires attention to all its parts. So it's obvious that understanding and changing social systems requires taking into account both the so-called public sphere of politics and economics and the so-called private sphere of family and other intimate relations.

Indeed, particular attention has to be paid to the social construction of gender and parent-child relations. The reason, simply put, is that it is in these primary human relations; the relations without which none of us would be here that people first learn to respect the rights of others to freedom from violence, cruelty, oppression, and discrimination, or to accept violence, cruelty, oppression, and discrimination as "just the way things are."

Leaving behind traditions of domination and violence in these foundational relations is essential for a more caring and just society. Yet this is still ignored in most writings about social justice – even though findings from psychology and neuroscience show that what children observe and/or experience profoundly affects their adult beliefs, behaviors, political attitudes, even the neural structures of their developing brains (Niehoff, 1999; Perry, 2010).

Fortunately, not all people raised in households where women and children are subjected to abuse, discrimination, and oppression accept human rights violations in the public sphere. But studies document that individuals who participate in and/or acquiesce to authoritarianism, violence, and scapegoating in the state or tribe tend to be individuals from families where authoritarianism, violence, and scapegoating were the norm (Adorno et al., 1964). These studies verify what common sense tells us: that the link between insensitivity, cruelty, and violence in the private sphere of the family and the public sphere of the state is all too real.

Yet none of our old social categories connect the dots between our intimate relations and our national and international relations. This is why in reporting the findings from my research I had to coin new terms to describe two contrasting social configurations that keep repeating themselves historically and cross culturally. I called one the *domination system* and the other the *partnership system*.

FROM DOMINATION TO PARTNERSHIP

I want to clarify that by partnership system I do *not* mean a completely flat organization. There are hierarchies, as there have to be – we need parents, teachers, managers, and leaders. But in partnership systems, these are not *hierarchies of domination* but *hierarchies of actualization*, used not to disempower, but to empower others. Nor do I mean just working together. People work together all the time in domination systems: terrorists cooperate, monopolies cooperate, invading armies cooperate.

By partnership system I mean a social configuration that has been struggling to emerge. The good news is that there is already strong movement in a partnership direction, albeit against enormous resistance and periodic regressions. In critical respects the European Middle Ages looked like the Taliban. Both are theocratic domination systems of rigid top-down rule in the family and state or tribe, rigid male dominance, and a high degree of violence in both the private or family sphere and the public sphere – be it witch burnings or public stonings of women, holy Crusades or holy Jihads. If there had not been movement toward the partnership side of the continuum, and it's always a matter of degree, we would not have concepts such as social justice and human rights, much less more recent concepts like women's rights and children's rights.

We clearly see this connection between a more equitable and caring society and women's and children's rights in the nations that today are closest to the partnership configuration: Nordic nations such as Sweden, Norway, Iceland, and Finland. The first part of this configuration is more democracy in *both* the family and the state, and there is no real democracy without both. The second is a major effort to leave behind traditions of violence in both intimate and international relations: for instance, the first peace studies came out of Nordic nations; so did a strong men's movement to disentangle "masculinity" from its association with control and violence and the first laws against physical disciplining of children in families. The third part of the partnership configuration is more equal partnership between the female and male halves of humanity.

Women are approximately 40 percent of national legislatures. And with this higher status of women came greater support, not only by women, but by men for more caring policies such as universal healthcare, stipends to help families care for children, elder care with dignity, and generous paid parental leave for both mothers and fathers.

These nations are also in the forefront of the movement toward a more environmentally sustainable economy. And countering the notion that they are more likely to care for their people because the population is more homogeneous they invest a higher percentage of their wealth than other "developed" nations in programs to help women, men, and children in the "developing world."

Of special significance in relation to a more socially just society, which these nations exemplify, they are *not* socialist, but a mix of market and centrally planned economies. Even more significant is that they often call themselves "caring societies."

SOCIAL JUSTICE AND CARING

Many people, including people who consider themselves progressives, still define social justice primarily in socialist or populist terms. But history demonstrates that if our aim is a society where the human rights and dignity of every human being are valued and respected regardless of race, religion, sex, ethnicity, or other differences, a new conceptual framework for social justice is needed.

Historic and cross-cultural data shows that cultures or subcultures where people are taught men should dominate women are also cultures where in-group versus out-group thinking, and with this, discrimination based on race, religion, and other differences is considered acceptable and even moral. For example, when Hitler came to power, a major goal was "returning women to their traditional place." Stalin saw to it that laws again labeled children born out of wedlock "illegitimate" and that efforts to change inequality in families, feeble though they had been, were abandoned. These are secular societies, but we see the same pattern in religious "fundamentalist" cultures or subcultures – be they Eastern or Western, Muslim or Christian.

All these are cultures where not only women but also anything considered "soft" or "feminine," be it in a woman or a man, is devalued. So caring, caregiving, and nonviolence are relegated to the same inferior status as women, and considered "unmanly" for "real men" (Eisler, 2008).

WHAT'S LEFT OUT OF THE SOCIAL JUSTICE DISCOURSE?

When we talk about building a more just society, these systems dynamics must be taken into account. Otherwise, social justice will continue to be an abstraction at best, and at worst misused.

Consider that rabid anti-Semites like the Catholic priest Father Coughlin supported Hitler's policies in the name of social justice, a term he trumpeted far and wide on radio and through his magazine *Social Justice*, where he blamed Jews for the Depression, atheism, and communism.

Even the famous definition of justice as fairness proposed by the philosopher John Rawls does not address the basics of empathy and caring. Couched in abstract principles of equality and freedom, Rawls's theory applies social justice to what he considered fundamental social institutions such as courts and markets with no consideration of what norms are inculcated by the institution most basic to socialization: the family. Nor is there a hint that matters connected with the majority of the population, women and children, merit consideration.

Unfortunately, this is hardly unusual, even though the statistics and the harrowing stories are all there. Globally, violence against women and children is the most ubiquitous violation of human rights. In many parts of Southeast Asia little girls are given less education, healthcare, and even food than boys. Genital mutilations of girls and women are still condoned by custom and religion in parts of Asia, Africa, and the Middle East, as are so-called honor killings (www.saiv.net, 2010). Yet these kinds of horrors are still generally ignored in the discourse about social justice and fairness.

A REDEFINITION OF SOCIAL JUSTICE

We humans have an inborn sense of fairness. But how we define what is fair largely hinges on the degree to which a culture of subcultures orients to the domination or partnership side of the continuum. And this, in turn, is directly related to what is considered normal and moral in our gender and parent-child relations. Of course, what we are dealing with is nothing inherent in women or men, but rather dominator gender stereotypes. We see this, in the men now doing fathering in the more hands-on caregiving way once associated only with mothering. But it's only as the status of women rises, as it did in Nordic nations, that men no longer feel so threatened in their status, in their "masculinity," when they embrace more stereotypically "feminine" values such as caring and nonviolence.

Cross-cultural studies show a strong correlation between the status of women and a nation's quality of life and long-term economic success. For instance, the Center for Partnership Studies compared statistical measures from 89 nations on the status of women with measures of quality of life such as infant mortality, human rights ratings, and environmental ratings (Eisler, Love, & Noorgard, 1995). We found that in significant respects the status of women can be a better predictor of quality of life than GDP. Other studies show the same, from the World Values Surveys to the World Economic Forum's Global Gender Gaps reports.

Policy-makers need this kind of information, and it's up to us to provide it. Take poverty and hunger. The U.S., which in the last decades backtracked on raising the status of women and at the same time failed to invest in caring for people, has the highest poverty rates of any industrialized nation. By contrast, Nordic nations, where the status of women is higher and caring is valued, have very low poverty rates.

Not only that, Nordic nations have very low poverty rates for woman-headed families, while the US has very high ones. Moreover, in the US women over the age of 65 are twice as likely to be poor as men over 65 according to US Census statistics. And this isn't just because of job discrimination, but because most of these women are or were caregivers, whether full or part time, and current policies do not reward, but rather punish this work with poverty. This is also a major reason that worldwide women are 70 percent of those living in absolute poverty, which means starvation or near starvation.

What all this points to is the need for a new inclusive definition of social justice. I propose that we define social justice as characteristic of societies that invest in caring for their people's basic material needs and protect human rights and human dignity in all relations, from intimate to international (Eisler, 1987; 1996). I also propose that social justice is impossible in societies that orient primarily to a domination system, where difference, beginning with the most basic difference in our species between female and male is equated with superiority or inferiority, dominating or being dominated, being served or serving.

We must redefine social justice to include both halves of humanity and both the so-called public and private spheres, thereby finally including the most vulnerable among us. This redefinition can lead to a new kind of revolution: the caring revolution urgently needed to build a world where all children – both girls and boys – can realize their enormous human potentials.

EXTENSION QUESTIONS/ACTIVITIES

1. Is the sole purpose of social justice to shine light on oppressed groups or peoples who are discriminated against?

2. Is the only way to achieve social justice through revolution and reform?

3. How can we define social justice if the meaning of justice differs from culture to culture?

4. Eisler proposes that we define social justice as characteristic of societies that invest in caring for their people's basic material needs and protect human rights and human dignity in all relations, from intimate to international (Eisler, 1987, 1996). She also proposes that social justice is impossible in societies that orient primarily to a domination system, where difference, beginning with the most basic difference in our species between female and male is equated with superiority or inferiority, dominating or being dominated, being served or serving. Review some of the main points from Riane Eisler's article, and then in writing, react to her definition. Be prepared to share your reaction with colleagues in a small group or with the entire class.

REFERENCES

Adorno, T. W., Frenkel-Brunswick, E., Levinson, D., & Nevitt Stanford, R. (1964). *The authoritarian personality*. New York: John Wiley & Sons.

Eisler, R. (August 1987). Human rights: Toward an integrated theory for action. *The Human Rights Quarterly*, 9(3).

Eisler, R., Love, D., & Noorgard, K. (1995). *Women, men, and the global quality of life*. Pacific Grove, CA: Center for Partnership Studies.

Eisler, R. (1996). Human rights and violence: Integrating the private and public spheres. In L. Kurtz & J. Turpin (Eds.), *The web of violence*. Urbana, IL: University of Illinois Press.

Eisler, R. (1998). *The chalice and the blade: Our history, our future*. San Francisco, CA: Harper & Row.

Eisler R. (2007). *The real wealth of nations: Creating a caring economics*. San Francisco, CA: Berrett Koehler Publishers.

Niehoff, D. (1999). *The biology of violence*. New York: Free Press.

Perry, B. (2010). Aggression and violence: The neurobiology of experience. Retrieved, October 10, 2010 from: http://teacher.scholastic.com/professional/bruceperry/aggression_violence.htm. The Spiritual Alliance to Stop Intimate Violence. Retrieved, October 10, 2010 from: www.saiv.net.

Riane Eisler
Center for Partnership Studies

ROBERT RUEDA

CULTIVATING COMPASSION: LESSONS LEARNED FROM CLASSROOMS TO EDUCATIONAL RESEARCHERS

The term social justice is likely a contemporary equivalent of a Rorschach test, where one sees and defines it according to the constellation of experiences and people and meaning-making that constitute the totality of one's life. Therefore, if many people are asked to define social justice there will be many different definitions. Definitions would likely be based on a variety of factors, like political orientation, gender, race, ethnicity, religious background, political and social philosophy, and other considerations. Which of these is correct? While the present volume may provide some answers, it is more probable that, like "beauty," the definition is in the eyes of the beholder.

It is likely that most people hold a common understanding of justice in a legal context, even though that understanding might be occasionally shaken when controversial court cases are decided in favor of a defendant based on legal technicalities. However, while there may be some general consensus about the meaning of legal justice, that same clarity seems to fade away when the term "social" is substituted for "legal." When the notion of justice spills out of the well-defined boundaries of the legal system, with its voluminous and complex regulations, procedures, discourse, and cultural practices and in to the real world, the consensus seems to disappear.

At times, the controversy about the concept goes beyond simple disagreements about nuances in meaning to whether it is a viable or worthy concept at all. A recent news piece reported on the comments of a popular and highly visible conservative broadcaster related to social justice. The broadcaster suggested that any church promoting "social justice" or "economic justice" was using code words for Nazism and communism. The column quoted the broadcaster with the following statement: "I beg you to look for the words social justice or economic justice on your church Web site," he said. "If you find it, run as fast as you can. Social justice and economic justice, they are code words ... Am I advising people to leave their church? Yes!" While some of the emotional outburst was likely driven by entertainment-related theatrics, the core of the disagreement appears to be equating social justice with the re-distribution of wealth. It is clear that when social justice begins to intrude upon the economics of the social order or involves the potential for institutional or political involvement, the stakes (and the controversy) seem to rise accordingly. Likewise, when the questions around social

Louis G. Denti and Patricia A. Whang (eds.), Rattling Chains: Exploring Social Justice in Education, 59–65.
© 2012 Sense Publishers. All rights reserved.

justice turn to issues such as, *"Who should be responsible for making sure society is a just and fair place? How does one implement policies promoting social justice? Should government legislate for justice in society or merely rely on the compassion or good will of society?"* there is less consensus on the appropriate course of action.

Given this situation, it seems unrealistic to synthesize and analyze the many perspectives on social justice and attempt to provide the definitive perspective. In addition, in light of the complexity and ambiguity of the construct, as well as the limitations of the present piece, it seems that a more sensible approach might be to provide a personal perspective. Thus, rather than attempting to answer the question, "What is social justice?" I will attempt to answer the question, "What is *my* take on social justice?"

SOCIAL JUSTICE, LANGUAGE, IDENTITY, AND POLITICS IN THE CENTRAL CITY: A PERSONAL PERSPECTIVE

Much of my career has focused on work in schools or on work related to teaching and learning schools. It has been loosely defined by the intersection of issues related to culture, language, motivation, teaching, learning, and literacy. Most often, it has involved populations that by many accounts are those for whom social justice has been most elusive. These include students in poverty and in other at-risk conditions, students who are English Learners, students who are low achievers and students with "learning problems," either inside or outside of special education. My interest in these groups is related to the long-standing and systematic differences in academic and later life outcomes between these and other groups in society. These are students for whom social justice is more than an abstract concept; its presence or absence can mean the difference between dramatically different life outcomes.

For individuals, a social justice perspective can be seen as a commitment to not obstruct the opportunities of others and to commit to helping maximize those opportunities where possible. For institutions and organizations, it is the equivalent of in individual's responsibility to consider the consequences of their actions. There are many lenses that might be brought to bear – political and economic, to name a few (as noted above) – but a constant in the discussion around social justice seems to center around assuring that no systematically negative impacts on any group or individual result from systematic or deliberate policies and activities. It may help to bring these abstract ideas to a real-world educational context.

There are two incidents from my research in classrooms that have left strong impressions on me and have stayed with me over time. Each of these speaks at some level to the issue of social justice and education. I describe each of them below.

Why don't they like our language?

A few years back, I joined a group of researchers in a national center effort focused on the area of reading. I, and a team of colleagues at the university embarked on a series of studies that were focused on inner-city immigrant students. I was particularly interested in issues related to motivation and reading. We focused our work at a community educational and social service agency and a public school that were located close to each other in the center of the city. Many of the families worked in the garment and other factories in the downtown area, virtually all students lived in poverty, and almost all were Spanish-speaking and immigrants. This particular school and community center were located near the Main Street section of the city that traditionally had been the area where the homeless congregated. One of the things that distinguished this school, at the time that we worked there, is that it had one of the largest numbers of homeless students in the country. While some students traveled with their parents on the bus as they came from the surrounding area to work, many more lived in the cheap hotels and shelters in the surrounding neighborhoods. Some students slept in the family car and others did not know where they would be staying the following evening. The continuing threat of deportation, fueled by immigration raids on downtown factories, was a constant source of anxiety for many of the families.

The circumstances of this school are not unique in that they can be found in many urban schools. In spite of depressing surroundings, there were indeed bright spots to be found. One teacher in particular drew our attention because of her approach to her classroom and the students within. While many of the classrooms were full of students working on endless drills and worksheets, one classroom stood out. In this classroom, students were active, engaged, and collaborating. There was a strong sense of collaboration, democracy, inquiry, and exploration. This particular class was a good example of the implementation of the "funds of knowledge" work (Gonzalez, Moll, & Amanti, 2005), which sees students' everyday experiences and out of school cultural practices and knowledge as cultural resources to build on for instructional purposes. While the teacher was not familiar with the theoretical vocabulary and concepts associated with the theory, she was a great example of how to put it to practice. She took great pains to know as much as she could about the students and their families, and then use that as a starting point for the academic content in the classroom. She made every effort to form good relationships with students and their families, and to engage parents in their children's' education. While many schools serving similar populations complain about the lack of parent involvement, the meetings and activities that she carried out for parents were often full.

The classroom reflected the perspective the teacher held related to the education of her students in which they were active partners. The room was full of reading materials and books that the teacher had acquired or purchased on her own. Students were often observed working in pairs or small groups or reading or worked on projects and, as this was a bilingual classroom, classroom business was carried on in English and Spanish as the situation called for. The contrast between this class and the others at the school could not have been more evident.

At the time that we were carrying on the study at this school, there was a statewide vote on a Voter Initiative regarding the issue of curtailing bilingual education. It was a highly contentious and publicized debate, in part fueled by anti-immigrant sentiment and the state's economic difficulties. For a variety of reasons, this particular school became a symbol of the controversy in a very public fashion, with a great deal of media attention, demonstrations, etc.

During one of the classroom visits, after one of the debates had taken place, one of the research team members overheard a young girl in the class ask, "Why don't they like our language?" in reference to the pointed attacks in the media and elsewhere related to bilingual education and immigrants. It was clear that in this curious and inquisitive child's mind, the debates were no longer a social and political abstraction, but a personal matter that went to the very heart of her identity as a person. Rather than trying to shield the students from all of the discord and controversy, the teacher made it an object of study in which the children could engage the controversy at their level of understanding. She organized debates in which students would argue one side or the other in order that they could see and think about the issues on their own. It was clear that this teacher took great care to value and to integrate her students' language and culture in to the classroom, both before and after this specific incident, and gave these students every opportunity to deal with these unsettling circumstances in a respectful and educationally beneficial fashion in spite of the difficult circumstances. Yet one has to wonder how many other children in similar circumstances were not so fortunate to have this type of social mediation available to them, and what the concept of social justice might have to offer in this educational context.

Passing as English-fluent

At the beginning of my career in academia many years ago, one of the issues I was concerned with was the problem of overrepresentation of African American and Latino students in certain special education categories. During this period, there did not exist the legal protections, due process, and procedural safeguards regarding student testing and special education diagnosis that exist today. Students could be placed in special education on the basis of tests alone. In that early work, it quickly became evident that standardized assessments were problematic for many students who came to school and to testing situations with different life experiences than those typically reflected on the tests and in the classroom. It also became evident that while issues of culture and context played an important role in trying to understand this problem, there was little discussion of these areas in the literature at the time.

In the search for more relevant perspectives with which to address this problem, I spent a year as a postdoctoral fellow at the Laboratory for Comparative Human Cognition (LCHC) at the University of California, San Diego. Michael Cole, the director, and his colleagues had done significant work in trying to understand culture and context related to cognitive functioning and behavior (e.g., Cole & Bruner, 1971; Cole, Gay, Glick, & Sharp, 1971). During my tenure there, I spent part of the time working on a project looking at students' reading behavior in both classroom and in specially created after-school settings. I was fortunate to be able to collaborate with a sociologist, Bud Mehan, who was affiliated with the lab, on a splinter study. We spent the better part of a year interacting with and observing a middle elementary Latino student, Miguel, who was labeled as learning disabled at school. As observations confirmed, in class Miguel was a poor reader, to the extent that other "poor readers" in the class mocked his reading. Given what we understood about the influence of context, we were interested in tracking his reading practices across various contexts – from the most formal and constrained (at school and in testing situations) to the least formal and constrained (at home and in the community). We expected that we might find expertise in reading or literacy activities outside of school that was not manifested at school. We found (Rueda & Mehan, 1986), however, that indeed Miguel was poor both in *and* outside of school. In fact, we found that he spent a great deal of time and effort, in often very clever ways, avoiding reading and situations in which his low skills might be revealed. We described his surprising expertise as an example of "passing and management," borrowing from Goffman's (1963) work on stigma with mental patients and their attempts to appear normal.

Almost twenty-five years later, I had the opportunity to work on a study looking at reading-based instructional issues with Latino immigrant students (Monzo & Rueda, 2009). Part of the study involved observations of students during their very structured reading time. At the time of the study, two important factors impacted classroom practices. First, bilingual instruction was formally halted in the state, except in very limited situations. Second, low performing schools such as this particular school, were required to use a very structured and scripted reading program that was designed for English speaking students. Our conversations with students over the course of the study suggested that there was a very high premium placed on the ability to speak English. Our conversations with students also revealed (as did our observations) that they were engaging in strategic behaviors in the classroom designed to disrupt the lesson or in other ways deflect the teacher's attention away from the fact that they were not competent in English and simply were not able to engage the academic content. Rather than allow their limited English speaking skills to become a target for public ridicule, they used various strategies to engage in passing and management activities that were highly reminiscent of those of Miguel decades earlier, but in an entirely new context.

LESSONS LEARNED

At the beginning of the article, I promised to provide my perspective on social justice, a personal perspective centered on the issue of social justice in education. It is a perspective colored by the above examples and many other similar ones not mentioned here. What can one take away from these seemingly unrelated stories? Perhaps they provide *counter-examples* – that is, examples of what social justice in education is *not*. I often wonder about the students in these examples and where they are today, and how many others like them can be found in today's classrooms. From my perspective, the examples reinforce those definitions of social justice calling for equality of opportunity and the notion that education should provide a foundation and support for making choices that maximize each individual's unique

63

gifts and talents. It certainly encompasses the notion of *opportunity to learn* (Stevens & Grymes, 1993). It means providing a setting where students do not need to feel ashamed of whom they are or the language they or their parents speak allowing for a range of abilities such that students' identities or self-efficacy are not damaged because of things they have not yet mastered. It also means shifting from the view that "We taught it, they should have learned it" that is found in some schools to one of taking responsibility for maximizing student learning no matter what point of the latter they enter at, and providing basic things like a safe environment, high expectations, and qualified and respectful teachers. Does it mean that all students be guaranteed equally positive outcomes? No – but it does mean that the *possibility* of positive outcomes is not limited by virtue of where one is located on the social or economic ladder. However, beyond these notions of equality, I join others (Ladson-Billings & Tate, 1995; Moje, 2007) who distinguish between "socially just pedagogy" which focuses only on equality of opportunity, and "social justice pedagogy." This latter perspective includes not only access to core knowledge and practices, as noted above, but also provide opportunities to question, challenge, and reconstruct knowledge such that the social and political contexts in which learning and other social action (such as the creation of educational inequalities in the first place) occur are open to examination.

While these are only a few of the many aspects of social justice in education that might be included here, it is clear that however narrowly one defines it, it is lacking for an unacceptable number of students in our schools. It is true that the immediate benefits of a social justice perspective toward education may benefit the individual; however, the ultimate cost to the larger society is much greater when it is lacking.

EXTENSION QUESTIONS/ACTIVITIES

1. Rueda indicates how one defines or experiences social justice is in the eye of the beholder. Where does your definition of social justice come from?

2. Rueda contends that education should call for equality of opportunity in order to provide a foundation and support for making choices to maximize each individual's unique gifts and talents. It seems as if equality in education as a foundation for choice making is on shifting sand; some students maximize their potential while others, because of circumstances pointed out by Rueda, do not even come close to realizing their potential. In fact, many dreams and aspirations are squashed. Why do schools portend and pretend to be socially just yet inequities appear so blatant? Is social justice pedagogy a luxury nowadays when scripted programs rule the day? Discuss these two questions in a small group and come up with ways your classroom or school has or can lay the foundation for equality of opportunity.

3. Do you question the status quo and some practices that are antithetical to your beliefs at your school or have you given into consciously or

unconsciously to the adage, "That's the way it is, that's the way it's always going to be."

REFERENCES

Cole, M., & Bruner, J. S. (1971). Cultural differences and inferences about psychological process. *American Psychologist, 26*(10), 867-876.

Cole, M., Gay, J., Glick, J. A., & Sharp, D. W. (Eds.). (1971). *The cultural context of learning and thinking.* New York: Basic Books.

Goffman, E. (1963). *Stigma: Notes on the management of spoiled identity.* Englewood Cliffs, NJ: Prentice-Hall.

Gonzalez, N., Moll, L., & Amanti, C. (2005). *Funds of knowledge: Theorizing practice in households, communities, and classrooms.* Mahwah, NJ: Lawrence Erlbaum.

Ladson-Billings, G., & Tate, W. (1995). Toward a critical race theory of education. *Teachers College Record, 97,* 47-68.

Monzo, L., & Rueda, R. (2009). Passing as English fluent: Latino immigrant children masking language proficiency. *Anthropology & Education Quarterly, 40*(1), 20-40.

Rueda, R., & Mehan, H. (1986). Metacognition and passing: Strategic interactions in the lives of students with learning disabil-ities. *Anthropology and Education Quarterly, 17*(3), 145-165.

Siegel, H. (2010). Christians rip Glenn Beck over "social justice" slam. *ABC News.* Retrieved from http://abcnews.go.com/WN/glenn-beck-social-justice-christians-rage-back-nazism/story?id= 10085008.

Stevens, F. I., & Grymes, J. (1993). *Opportunity to learn: Issues of equity for poor and minority students.* Washington, DC: National Center for Education Statistics.

Robert Rueda
University of Southern California

RONALD DAVID GLASS

CULTIVATING COMPASSION: LESSONS LEARNED FROM COMMUNITY AND FAMILY

In this essay, I explore social justice through some of my youthful formative experiences in the 1950s and 1960s, and through some of my novice teaching efforts in transformative pedagogy in the early 1970s. I conclude with some comments about learning about social justice though everyday experience.

As a child, I learned most deeply about social justice through my experiences of injustice – coupled with the subsequent interpretations of those experiences provided by my parents and other trusted elders – and through my own and my family's efforts to confront injustice and live our lives in ways congruent with our ethical, religious, and political commitments. My motivation to take my place in the long march toward a more just society emerged initially from my anger at being treated unfairly, at being discriminated against because I was Jewish, but as I grew up, I learned that others also suffered from a world in which inordinate power and privilege were held by white, male, wealthy Christians.

Shortly before I entered second grade in the mid-1950s, my family moved to a small northwest Ohio industrial and farming town firmly in the grip of John Birch Society ideology and political apparatus. We broke a 'color-line' to become the first Jewish family to buy a house and live in the best school district, and remained the only such family in that district for nearly ten years. School recess became a daily test of wills as some kids harassed me, or called me derogatory names; my verbal combat skills meant that some kids needed to resort to physical intimidation to maintain their sense of superiority. Other kids found quieter ways to enforce the social boundaries, often simply by not including me; during my first six years attending school there, I was invited to another kid's house only one time. While these well-aimed attacks and slights hurt me, they were not my most painful and vivid experiences of injustice at school.

I knew that kids could be cruel and unfair, and that this need not have any relationship to my Jewish identity. After all, when my extended family got together for holidays or vacations, my cousins and I certainly enacted our own full measure of wrongs on each other; but our occasional mean-spirited play drew loud condemnations from the adults. The adjudication of our conflicts aimed both to punish the guilty and also to instruct us in the good, in the expectations of a moral life. Lessons delivered at Hebrew School reinforced these expectations, and conjured a watchful and sometimes wrathful G*d whose people revere justice and live in exemplary ways. At school, however, precisely the lack of such condemnations and adjudications from the adults marked that particular public

Louis G. Denti and Patricia A. Whang (eds.), Rattling Chains: Exploring Social Justice in Education, 67–72.
© 2012 *Sense Publishers. All rights reserved.*

sphere as profoundly unjust, as a domain in which serious threats to my moral sensibilities were as prevalent as the daily threats to my physical and psychological well being. The adults held the power at school. Yet there, unlike at home or at the synagogue, racist and anti-Semitic comments, jokes, or actions often went unremarked upon and unpunished.

This coupling of power with morally blameworthy actions constituted my first real experiences with injustice. At school, I began to realize that I and other innocents were accepted targets of discrimination, and that those who targeted us would rarely suffer any consequences for their actions. One day, my 7th grade math teacher kept me after class to harangue me about my family and Jewishness, clearly even more of an affront to him than my perfect performance in class as he repeatedly failed to catch me out in an error. I was terrified, and even now, fifty years later, the memory stirs my heart. When I told my parents on arriving home, they immediately called the principal to complain. The next day he questioned me closely, and challenged me with the teacher's denial. Luckily a girl from my neighborhood whose father was a gutsy defense attorney had heard it all from the classroom doorway, and her brave testimony corroborated my account. The principal called the teacher to the office and forced him to apologize to me; yet Mr. B remained my teacher and graded me unfairly whenever he could get away with it. A year later, the discovery that I would have to go to his house to be examined for my Boy Scout Scholarship Merit Badge prompted an intense debate within my family, but ultimately I steeled myself for this disgusting experience and preserved my dignity in the midst of it. In high school, the most noxious abuse I suffered was being paddled with a wooden board in front of crowds of students for exceedingly minor offenses or no offense at all. For example, my junior year I was paddled on a platform in front of a study hall, with all one hundred or so students purposefully kept after school for a few minutes for the display. My sin had been to whisper, "you dropped your pencil," to a girl hurriedly packing up in anticipation of the bell and the rush to catch the bus.

Through such school experiences, I learned to marshal my courage to speak truth to power, and to stand up for myself no matter the risk; but I also learned that injustice withstands individual resistance almost unscathed. Other experiences taught me that my family and our small Jewish community (about one hundred families) could also be assaulted with seeming impunity. Vandals broke into our synagogue to desecrate it with swastikas and cause property damage; fewer than fifteen years after the end of the Holocaust, this incident powerfully impressed my young mind and affirmed my family's frequent reminders of the fragility of Jewish existence. When my parents provided support to a new weekly newspaper meant to counter the right wing 'daily news' we started finding the dominant newspapers strewn across our dew soaked yard every morning. The attempts to intimidate and silence us did not succeed, and as time went along, I began to see that it was possible to fight back, with power, money, and organization.

My parents hired a "big city" lawyer to come to town to defend a Pentecostal church attended by our housekeeper when it suffered eviction pressures from an unscrupulous landlord and no local attorney would aid them, cementing our proudly embraced reputation as "nigger lovers." When the church eventually built its own place of worship, they honored my family on the engraved cornerstone. It was no surprise when my parents threatened to sue a person who nominated my family for membership at the elite country club that excluded Jews and Blacks; he had not secured my parents' permission to use my family to break that color-line, and it was important that everyone in the community understand that we had absolutely no interest in joining such odious company. Similarly, my parents became business partners with two gay men (in a long-term 'married' relationship) whose aspirations to be restaurant owners and cooks, far exceeding the capacity of their tiny (ironically named) *Dairy Queen* franchise, had been thwarted by the refusal of the banks to support their enterprise. Together they opened a thriving mid-scale restaurant in a stunning building designed by a leading architect from the state capital.

These actions gave force to the countless dinner table conversations that analyzed the injustices of the day, and made me highly conscious of both my obligations and my privileges. I also knew that we were not perfect as individuals or as a family, and that we ourselves embodied some of the very injustices we battled against. Class-based negative judgments were not uncommon among my grandparents and parents, and these were used to spur us children toward diligent study and hard work; yet they also aroused unease with their pejorative generalizations. Gender roles were clear-cut, even amidst contradictory expectations. I was formally relieved of daily family kitchen duty when I turned sixteen (though thereafter expected to be largely self-sufficient); at the same time, I was drilled with the necessity of respecting women, and my sisters were expected to become educated and even have careers. And of course, any hint of hypocrisy in our grandparents and parents occasioned our intense self-righteous criticism of them along with numerous loud arguments at those same dinner tables.

Before finishing high school, I got my first sense of being part of a larger movement for justice in the U.S. when my parents and I joined a small contingent of local civil rights marchers in solidarity with those in Selma, AL, who faced down the violent racists there. The intense hatred of the onlookers who yelled and spat at us made me viscerally realize the great distance to be traveled to transform our community and the nation. In college, my nascent activism became more deeply engaged in my opposition to the Viet Nam war. In October 1967, at the first large Pentagon demonstration and national draft card burning, I experienced the shock of armed U.S. troops, with bayonets fixed on their rifles, assaulting peaceful protesters. I fully grasped for the first time that I was a person in history, that my choices and actions made a difference not just for me but also for everyone. I shifted my career plans from medical school toward an unknown path, moved only by my growing commitment to devote my life to the struggle for justice. I opted to become an educator, hoping that the transformation of schooling could leverage history and open up a more just and humane future.

Inspired by Paulo Freire's *Pedagogy of the Oppressed*, I made social justice central to my two student teaching assignments, one at a working class neighborhood elementary school and the other at a special one-year program for students expelled from Boston area high schools (many of whom attended the program on day-release from jail). For the teenagers, I taught a class titled "What is a Human Being?" that critiqued their everyday lives to illuminate the structural forces at work in their seemingly personal choices to rebel and live outside the law. I discovered that their cognitive recognition of social-political realities did little to break the grip of dominant ideologies, and that the school and 'criminal justice' system forces nearly always trumped the progressive content and dialogical dynamics of my classroom. With the teacher's encouragement in my 3rd-4th grade class, I gathered up the "Gang of 9" boys who were perpetually truant and repeatedly suspended and we set up our own space in a basement room by the furnace. There we constructed a large neighborhood 'map' that consolidated our research about the community and our observations gleaned on lengthy walks; the 'map' revealed the class and race relations embedded in the identities of the block-by-block segregated populations, of the local jail inhabitants, and of the occupants of the cars and buses leaving the neighborhood for jobs either downtown to the office towers or out to the factories on the community perimeter. Suddenly dutiful students arriving early to the school and happy to stay after on occasion as well, the boys were amazed to find explanations for their lived experience that did not cast them as deviant, troublemaking, nobodies. They also were amazed to learn a bit about broader social, economic, and political powers shaping their neighborhood and the everyday lives of their families. And I learned that a little social justice pedagogy was fine for a few kids – the teacher and principal were happy as long as I kept these students out of the classroom and detention office – but not so welcome as a curriculum for all students in the school. Even social justice struggles could be tokenized, and ironically become props for the maintenance of the status quo.

My first full-time teaching position was as the head teacher of an 'alternative' elementary school in California. I constructed virtually the entire curriculum around short 'mini-courses' based on students' interests, from oceanography and tide pools, to theater arts, gardening, classic literature, skateboarding, and even advanced algebraic equations. One memorable social justice oriented instructional unit got developed around my frustrations with all the candy consumed and candy wrappers strewn about the classrooms and playground: we deconstructed the political economy of a Snickers Bar. For each ingredient, students traced its global origins, determined the wages and standard of living of the workers who produced it, examined the economic and political structures of the exporting countries, calculated the profits generated for the multi-national corporation owning the candy-bar, and identified the health and dental consequences of over-indulgence in candy eating. To deconstruct the trash aspect of my frustrations, the students took a trip to the city dump, catalogued the types of trash piled mountainously high there, and interviewed the workers who collected and managed the waste. I don't believe any of this altered the kids' candy consumption, though it did for a time reduce the littering around the school; I am confident the experience made the students more ecologically aware and more cognizant of their location within a global political economy that privileged them. After two years as the leader of this school, I learned that alternatives may not always be so different from the standard fare –we teachers insured that students acquired the core academic competencies, even if exams and grades were replaced by more authentic assessments – and that it was mostly already advantaged students who received the benefit from such schools.

So at the end of these stories, what can I say about learning about social justice from our everyday experience? Such learning of course is no more straightforward than other kinds of learning, and it benefits enormously from the facilitation of a caring and knowledgeable teacher. Moreover, this kind of learning can only be fully realized when it becomes integrated with action that seeks to overcome the limits of situations and of our selves, and it is a kind of learning that must be re-learned again and again as our situations and our selves change. I also learned that social justice itself is similarly dynamic, that it is not a state of affairs that can be fully defined or achieved once and for all. Rather, social justice is constituted in a way of life, one embodied in the day-to-day struggle for equitable treatment and opportunity for all. What this means in each particular domain of existence can only come to be known in these very processes of struggle, processes of deliberation and contestation that seek to define meanings – what exactly is fair or equitable in a specific instance? – and realize those meanings in particular ways of life that are always historically and culturally situated, subject to further critique and revision.

We know for certain that seemingly natural, taken for granted states of affairs that at one time and place comprise the common sense way of living for a people, can become seen through the critical lens of struggle as intolerable, as conditions necessary to be challenged and changed. In the relatively short history of the U.S., we witnessed such struggles and changes in regard: to slavery and to civil rights for Blacks and other people of color; to the social, political, and legal status of women; to the rights of the differently-abled; and to the social and legal status of gay, lesbian, bi/transsexual people. We don't know exactly how history will judge our present age. But we do know that there are many people who continue the struggle on all these past fronts since victory over injustice is never complete. The persistent human appetite for power brings dehumanization, inequity, and iniquity in its wake, constrained and transformed only by the deep human will to extend the reach of the struggle for justice into ever more public spaces in civil society as well as the intimate spaces of everyday life often hidden from view. We also know that some people take up new causes in the name of justice, whether on behalf of non-human animals or plants, and the earth itself, or on behalf of the rights of children to quality educations and adequate health care and nutrition. If we care about social justice, and if we hope to learn from our own everyday experience, we are called to take our particular place in history and shoulder our share of the burden of these struggles. We make social justice as we live it.

EXTENSION QUESTIONS/ACTIVITIES

1. In Glass's essay he talks about marshalling courage to speak truth to power and to stand up for oneself no matter the risk. He also learned that

injustice withstands individual resistance almost unscathed. Jot down a time when you stood up for yourself, however the injustice persisted. Did you give up? Did you continue to fight? What feelings persist to this day? Share your thoughts with a partner or in a small group.

2. Class based negative judgments continue to part of daily conversations. When you encounter pejorative generalizations about class how do you respond? Are you at times hypocritical; meaning you detest class-based distinctions yet find yourself complicit, either through humor or not railing against off-putting stereotypical and discriminatory comments?

3. Glass says, "We make social justice as we live it." After reading his article talk about how social justice emanates from your own experience(s).

Ronald David Glass
University of California, Santa Cruz

MARA SAPON-SHEVIN

CULTIVATING COMPASSION: TEACHING OUR CHILDREN TO THINK AND ACT FOR SOCIAL JUSTICE

What is social justice and why does it matter? I could answer these questions in many ways: I could respond as a University professor who teaches courses in social justice, or as a peace activist who stands on corners handing out leaflets and holding up signs relating to various commitments to peace and justice concern ranging from peace in the Middle East to the environmental dangers of hydrofracking. I have chosen, instead, to write from another salient identity – that of being a mother – speaking from the places in which my larger world view and understandings of issues of equity, justice and fairness have intersected with my parenting and my desire to teach my children particular frameworks for thinking about their world and their places in it. I write from the voice of a parent/educator, hoping to articulate some of the "big ideas" about social justice that have emerged and been shaped by my experiences as a mother, offering eight questions that I propose we might want all children (and, by extension, all people) to think about on a daily basis. I ground these questions in stories of times in which these lessons became significant to me as a parent or a child and situations in which this principle was enacted – or absent. I am hopeful that these eight will provide a starting discussion for other questions and an exploration of the complexity of the questions themselves.

There are no simple questions and no easy answers; what there *can* be is a commitment to unpacking the questions and making them more and more challenging and exploring the difficulty of answering them. A student once wrote a critical evaluation of my course that said, "The problem with this course is that it's raised more questions than it's answered. At this point in my life I want answers, not more questions." I still treasure that evaluation because, although the student was clearly frustrated, I feel that I must have done a good job and I only hope that student is still finding more and more questions s/he thinks need answers.

A poem by the poet Rainer Marie Rilke's poem is on my wall, and it is a constant reminder to me of the importance of questions. It reads:

> Be patient toward all that is unsolved in your heart and try to love the questions themselves, like locked rooms and like books that are now written in a very foreign tongue. Do not now seek the answers, which cannot be given you because you would not be able to live them. And the point is, to live everything. Live the questions now.

Louis G. Denti and Patricia A. Whang (eds.), Rattling Chains: Exploring Social Justice in Education, 73–78.
© 2012 *Sense Publishers. All rights reserved.*

Perhaps you will then gradually, without noticing it, live along some distant day into the answer.

My questions are as follows:

How carefully are you paying attention to what surrounds you and what would it take for you to look a little more deeply? How do you name your world?

As parents and educators, we are often deeply uncomfortable with children's questions: "Why does that man have a cane? How come some kids in our school just have chips for lunch? Why aren't all the kids in our class going on the field trip? When will I get to go to the gifted program? Our discomfort often comes from the fact that as adults we have learned not to notice, not to mention, not to name the things we see around us – have been encouraged not to see, not to comment about. We all started out inquisitive and interested, but in the name of comfort, politeness and not making waves, we have been silenced. And so, in contrast, I want to cultivate in my children a stance of "wide-awakeness" a phrase coined by educator Maxine Greene that refers not just to awareness but to a willingness to DO something. I want my children to have a particular way of paying attention to and naming their world and the situations in which they find themselves. I don't want people to become invisible to them – the homeless woman on the street, the elder struggling to open the door, the child who uses a wheelchair. I don't want them to be afraid to name their observations. Certainly I want to teach them tact and kindness, but I want them to pay attention.

When one of my daughters was in elementary school, her teacher told us "Your daughter cares too much about other children." When we queried what that meant, the teacher explained that when another child broke his pencil and started to cry, our daughter went into her desk and gave him one of *her* pencils. The teacher said, "I told her, just do your own work and ignore other children." I was deeply troubled – I want my children to pay attention, to wonder what's happening, to think about possible reactions or responses. I have friends who always stop – as witnesses – when they see someone being detained by police, just to make sure that everything is happening in a respectful and appropriate way. They are attentive to possible enactments of racism or sexism, ever vigilant on behalf of those who may be mistreated. And all of this begins with paying good attention

Who do you know? Who is in your life? Who are your friends? And who is missing from this list?

Because I deeply value diversity, I want to instill in my children an awareness of who they see and who they know and how both overt and more subtle segregations and discriminations play out right in front of their eyes. I want them to leave their own comfort zones in order to know people whom they perceive as "different" from themselves, to be delighted by new people and experiences, to be unafraid of the unfamiliar. When we lived in the Midwest in an extremely racially and religiously homogeneous community, my children noticed and commented that all of the students in their classes were white, and that almost all of them were Christian. As teenagers, they commented that all the students in the honors program were white and that the special education classrooms were almost all students of color and predominantly male. When we moved to a more racially mixed community, my younger daughter Leora asked, "How come everyone brags about how dark a tan they got in the summer and then they discriminate against people with dark skin?"

As a child, I was actively discouraged from getting to know children from other socio-economic groups. When I described meeting someone new, the first question I was asked was always, "What does her/his father do?" The classism (and sexism) became clear to me much later, and it now fills me with anger and a deep sadness about all the children I never got to know because they were judged "inferior," "dangerous," or somehow inappropriate as friends.

Having diverse friends is an essential precursor to working for social justice because if our relationships and experiences do not cross these boundaries, we often don't hear and don't know the realities (and struggles) of other people, and thus may not see the injustices and inequities that surround us. When I lived in North Dakota, a Native American friend sat at my kitchen table and cried about what was happening to her son in the local middle school. When I shared her story (and others) as part of an anti-racism initiative, I was told, "I've never heard those stories before," as a way of discounting or challenging their veracity. So if we don't notice that our relationships are sharply constrained by identities of race, class, gender, religion, ethnicity, language or sexual orientation, then we are unlikely to be aware of the ways in which our lives differ.

How might others tell the story of a particular event or circumstance in which you find yourself, and how is that story different from yours? Why does it matter?

I want my children to ask, almost reflexively, "Is there another side to this story?" Early on, our discussions of Columbus Day and Thanksgiving included sharing that not everyone views these holidays the same way. One of our Native American friends in North Dakota said of Thanksgiving: "Did you ever invite someone to dinner and they just wouldn't go home?" As we laughed at that comment, we also discussed that the conqueror and the conquered are unlikely to tell the story the same way. And that is because the victors typically write history; we often never even hear "another side of the story."

This is a fairly commonsense lesson for children, because unpacking their conflicts often involves articulating differing perspectives. Asking, "What would the other child say happened?" or "Do you think everyone in your class feels the same way about this?" can begin conversations about justice and unfairness. Even in situations in which they were the "winners" or the lucky ones, I wanted them to be aware that the child who didn't get the reading award or the person who wasn't invited to the party would probably feel quite differently about how the situation was structured or the policy enacted. How do we move past the question, "How was this for me?" to the question, "How was this for other people?"

Is what is happening in this particular arena or situation "fair" and how would you decide?

My children attended a camp with a strong commitment to social justice. What this meant at a practical level was that the children were actively engaged (amidst swimming and arts and crafts) in thinking about issues of fairness. There were, for example, no private food packages allowed at camp. When a parent sent a box of cookies, pretzels or candy, it was with the knowledge that the contents of the box would be shared equally among the campers in the bunk. When someone in the bunk was hungry, the group would decide to open something in the shared trunk and distribute the contents: two cookies each or a handful of m&m's per child. Parents who would balk at the idea of feeding "other peoples' children" were unlikely to choose this camp. For me, it was far more important that my child be in a setting in which the "haves" (those with parents who had the money and other resources to send food packages) did not watch the "have-nots" go without while they enjoyed their snacks. And the bunks in each cabin were assigned only after all the girls had arrived, and then, through negotiation and consensus, rather than privileging those who arrived earlier by car over those who took the bus as a group. Not only were these practices enacted, but the children also engaged in conversations about what was fair and what wasn't and became active consumers of that terminology and adept at analyzing novel situations using a rubric of fairness.

Is it fair that wealth and resources are not unevenly distributed in our country and the world? What are the patterns of discrimination and prejudice that are manifested in the unequal distribution? What might it be like if it were different? What stands in the way?

What should you do when you see a situation that is unfair or a person who is being treated badly? What more do you need to know in order to stand up for others better or take an informed stance?

When one daughter was in elementary school, she had a teacher who was sometimes extremely verbally abusive to the students in her class. We learned (long after it happened), that when the teacher started chiding a young boy with learning disabilities, telling him that he was a "baby" and that she was going to "go out and buy baby food" for him. Our daughter said to the teacher, "Mrs. W – don't say that to him – it's not nice." This kind of courage in a nine-year old is stunning and powerful. How do we cultivate that willingness to notice – and take a stand? One of my favorite children's books is *Say Something* by Peggy Moss which describes a young girl who is, at first, self-congratulatory about how she isn't one of the kids who makes fun of others in school. When she becomes the target of teasing, however, she realizes that silence is collusion and that not speaking up in the face of injustice isn't laudatory at all. A popular ABC television show, "What Would You Do?" raises similar challenges; people are observed as they witness prejudice and discrimination and the cameras record whether or not they intervene.

Who benefits and who loses from the way things are now? Who made the rules that you are asked to follow and who benefits or loses from the enforcement of those rules?

This question is intimately related to questions two and four because it asks us to think deeply about fairness and justice – and to include in that thinking a wide range of people. It involves examining the status quo for underlying discrimination. If the school rule is that only students with grade point averages above a B are allowed to play sports, what happens to the students whose academic backgrounds have been seriously compromised by poverty and lack of resources, but for whom sports are a place and a way to excel? If you can only go to the school prom with a date of the "opposite sex," I want my children to not only ask who made that rule and why, but what are the effects on students who have friends, but not a "date" or who have a "date" that is a member of the same sex.

When Dalia was in fourth grade, the gym teacher made a rule that the students could no longer play with jump ropes because the boys had been swinging them around and hitting people. Dalia was incensed and wrote a letter to the gym teacher telling him that the rule was unfair and targeted the girls because of the boys' misbehavior. She wrote: "The girls are the ones that are good at jumping rope and they like doing it. And now you've taken away the thing we're good at because the boys were being bad. That's not fair to the girls." Jump ropes were re-instated.

I want my children to be skeptical consumers of rules. When we went to a local water park for example, there were lots of rules. Some of these rules, like the one banning glass bottles, were clearly related to safety. But the rule that you could only buy food from the park's concession stands, was a rule about capitalism and money making for the park, that had the effect of also making the water park even less accessible for those with less money. I want my children to neither ignore all rules in the name of rebellion and individuality nor follow all rules without interrogating them. And I want the interrogation of rules and a critical examination of the status quo to grow to include an ever-widening set of situations and policies: housing, employment, access to resources and services and so on.

Could the world be any different than it is now, and if so, how?

In order to make things different, we must be able to imagine things as different. A critique of the status quo is important, but it's not enough. What would it be like if schools were places of caring and acceptance? What would it be like if there were no wars and people settled conflicts peacefully? What would it be like if there were no hunger and all people had access to healthy food? Rather than cut off discussions about alternatives, branding them childish fantasies, chiding my children to live in "the real world," I have always encouraged them to think about what a just and fair world would be like. Maxine Greene describes having a "social imagination" as the capacity to invent visions of what could be and to consider "the possibility of repair." The Jewish tradition of Tikkun Olam (repair of the world) is also rooted in thinking about how things should be – and how to get there.

Labeling someone's vision as "idealistic," is a way of discrediting it and devaluing it. We act as though "accepting the way things are" is a hallmark of maturity rather than a sign of surrender and despair. A healthy sense of indignation and the ability to picture things other than they are now is an important and powerful response to injustice and inequities and should be nourished and supported.

What is your role in making the world better and what kinds of relationships do you need to have to do that work?

And, finally, I want my children to not just critique the status quo and imagine it differently but to see themselves as playing active roles in making things better. A recent campaign related to homophobic bullying and violence is entitled "It Gets Better"; although the ads are well-intentioned, a parallel campaign called "We Make It Better" articulates that patience and hope are not the hallmarks of social change. We must actively pursue actions and policies that will actually change things. I want to encourage my children to know that there are many sites of struggle and involvement, and that while they can't do everything, they can do something. Treating others with kindness and integrity is no less valuable than standing on street corners in protest. And, in fact, unless we have developed and nurtured relationships with a wide range of people, our political actions are likely to be ill-informed and poorly articulated. We cannot be active allies for Muslims, for example, after the Islamaphobia of September 11th, unless we have relationships with people who practice Islam and can help us make sure that our intentions and support are appropriate, empowering and not charitable, authentic and not superficial. I want my children – and all people – to see themselves as active agents of change, not passive recipients of a world filled with strife and despair.

These are but eight questions of many, but I am hopeful they are a beginning. Good questions always provoke more questions; what other questions do you think we should be asking?

EXTENSION QUESTIONS/ACTIVITIES

1. If actions speak louder than words what do your actions communicate about your commitment to social justice?

2. Devise a social justice Code of Ethics with a small group of your classmates or colleagues. Be prepared to share your Code of Ethics with the class.

3. Can you be socially just without deeply valuing diversity?

Mara Sapon-Shevin
Syracuse University

LOU BROWN

CULTIVATING COMPASSION: LESSONS LEARNED FROM INDIVIDUALS WITH SIGNIFICANT INTELLECTUAL DISABILITIES

Before humans could speak, draw or write they had rules, determinants and propensities that guided actions and led to consequences that defined and delivered justice. Genes and other biological phenomena probably had the most influence on their actions. As groups evolved across the planet, so did theories, hypotheses, suggestions and commandments related to the nature and parameters of justice. For thousands of years the few who determined justice for the many were the strongest, the smartest and the most powerful. Sometimes they were magnanimous and sometimes they were mean spirited and brutal. In some cultures justice was actualized if an arm was cut off a person who stole a blanket. In others justice was winning a war and then forcing those conquered into slavery. Over time, cultures and the governments they established became more complex and were organized into components.

Local constructions of justice were then applied to commerce, schools, law, public gatherings and militaries. In addition, they were applied to increasing numbers of individuals with increasingly different characteristics. In many places components of justice enjoyed by males was extended to women and to citizens of other races and sexual orientations.

COMPASSIONATE, HUMANE AND SUPPORTIVE SOCIAL JUSTICE

We cannot choose when, how or with what we enter the world. Accidents of nature, social and economic circumstances and many other factors we cannot control or that we are not responsible for can limit our options and place great burdens upon our families, our fellow citizens and us. In such instances we are in need of the assistance of others who are better situated. We agree with those who refer to justice as an uncompromising virtue entwined with fairness (Rawls, 1999) and the equitable distribution of opportunities and other resources among community members. Central to these and most other egalitarian constructions is the notion that everyone has capabilities that must be honored with reasonable opportunities to realize them (Nussbaum, 2006; Terzi, 2008; Walker, 2006). Our construction of social justice is compassionate, humane and supportive in nature. The application of helpful and sharing egalitarian principles has led to the development of a wide array of taxpayer-supported social services in many

Louis G. Denti and Patricia A. Whang (eds.), Rattling Chains: Exploring Social Justice in Education, 79–85.
© 2012 *Sense Publishers. All rights reserved.*

countries. Unemployment and medical insurance, social security benefits, vocational rehabilitation services and universal public education are examples.

"Social justice" is an extremely seductive and robust construct for many who function from a variety of perspectives. Many feel good when they advocate for opportunity, fairness, individual freedom, dignity, worth and shared resources. Unfortunately, others advocate for what we consider social injustice. They claim that it is not their responsibility to pay for costly services for others; that individuals are personally responsible for their status and well being; that the unequal distribution of resources is natural and acceptable; that caring for others is voluntary and discretionary; that the role of government in the lives of individuals must be minimized; and, that it is extremely important they are taxed as little as possible. To individuals who cannot advocate for themselves or who have neither the voice nor the means to survive or live decent lives without the financial and other supports of others who are more endowed they say "Tough. Not my problem. So be it. Life is not fair."

We believe any credible construction of social justice must clearly acknowledge the humanity of individuals who might not be able to secure it by themselves and that everyone must have at least the minimums needed to survive and thrive. These minimums include, but are not limited to, food, shelter, medical care, education, personal privacy, opportunities to actualize meaningful choices and the means to travel about a community. Without these and related minimums, decent or socially just lives cannot be experienced. If we all have access to the minimums, then talents, skills, individual choices and other factors will determine how the additional fruits of society are distributed. To me, an equitable distribution of resources does not mean an equal distribution.

We love to hear about individuals who have taken risks, achieved much and realized hard earned rewards. We encourage them to enjoy their successes and salute them when they do. However, we feel those of us who have more than the minimums have a responsibility to set aside a portion of our bounties to assist others who are also deserving of decent lives. We can have our boats, time shared resort apartments, jewelry, stables of cars, fine wines and many other "things" we can afford, but we must not deny the basic minimums to others who are unable to actualize such options. In short, all we ask is that those of us with means help others live, simple, basic, ordinary lives.

INDIVIDUALS WITH SIGNIFICANT INTELLECTUAL DISABILITIES

For purposes here "disability" means not able to do something. If you can do every thing everyone else can, you are not considered disabled. Disabilities of all kinds are real and important parts of the human experience. Ultimately all families and individuals will be directly touched by the penetrating realities of some form of disability.

Twenty-five years ago in an essay entitled, "Then and Now" Brown (1986) addressed several important issues related to the lives of the lowest intellectually functioning one percent of our fellow citizens. One issue was the critical need to emphasize the "personhood" of those individuals. Why? Because at that time, most claimed license to refer to and treat them as syndromes, objects, vegetables, less than human and diseases that did not have the rights and protections afforded those who were more intellectually able. They were segregated, sterilized, denied medical treatment, shocked with electricity, taken away from their families and loved ones, secluded even in segregated settings, restrained, denied access to public schooling and otherwise treated in ways we consider "socially unjust." No longer could we tolerate one group realizing close approximations of lives that are "socially just" and concurrently accept the unjust treatment of others. No longer could their humanity or capacities be denied, minimized or ignored. It was hoped that by emphasizing and demanding the acknowledgement of "personhood," more constructive and humane expectations, values, goals, pressures and opportunities would evolve into normalized protections and decent lives within integrated communities. Since 1986, much progress has been made. Almost all of the lowest intellectually functioning one percent of citizens in the United States under age twenty two are now experiencing taxpayer supported educational and related services (Alper & Wehmeyer, 2002). Each year more and more are performing real work in the real world (Brown, Shiraga, & Kessler, 2006). The numbers who live in public and private "institutions" has been reduced from over 350,000 to less than 40,000 (Rizzolo et al., 2004). Small but increasing numbers are living in apartments with not more than one other person with disabilities.

Increasing numbers of individuals with significant disabilities, in concert with family members and others, are demonstrating the abilities to make choices that lead to remarkable achievements in integrated employment, residential and general community environments and activities.

What is compassionate, human and supportive social justice for an eight-year-old girl with Down syndrome who is among the lowest intellectually functioning one percent of individuals her age? In 1929, her life expectancy would have been nine years. In 2012, it is around forty-two. She attends the same school and classes she would if she was not intellectually disabled. In her integrated school and classes she enjoys the benefits of individually appropriate extra supports, without which she would not be able to benefit from the activities she experiences. (Extra support refers to that which an individual with disabilities needs in order to survive and to thrive that she/he would not need if not disabled.) She lives at home with her mom, dad, sister and brother. She participates in integrated activities with her family in their faith community. She is involved in integrated swimming classes at the local YMCA. She is an enthusiastic member of a Girl Scout troop with her sister and neighbors. She enjoys sleepovers with her classmates who are and are not disabled. She goes to integrated Girl Scout camp each summer. She ...

She could not function effectively in these safe and enhancing integrated environments and activities without the assistance of family members, teachers, paraprofessionals, therapists, taxpayers and other members of her community. In the recent past she would have been denied access to public schooling, confined to a segregated " institution" or left to sit at home all day. Her life is not perfect, but it is relatively good. Now we must ensure it remains so, because when she exits public school and when her parents die, she will rely on all of us for different kinds and amounts of extra support.

COST

One of the reasons it is hard for many to consider the provision of individualized extra supports in integrated settings and activities as the best option for individuals with disabilities is because the majority of those who appropriate and allocate the necessary financial and other resources have rarely interacted with them directly and frequently over long periods of time. If individuals with significant intellectual disabilities grew up in integrated society, all members therein would get to know them and would understand the extra support they need. Then, the vast majority of taxpayers, legislators, business leaders, co-workers, neighbors and others would join the quest for compassionate, humane and supportive social justice to be actualized in their lives.

> What is compassionate, humane and supportive social justice for a seventeen-year old young man with autism who is among the lowest intellectually functioning one percent of all students in his school district? He attends the same high school he would attend if he were not intellectually disabled. In his school and classes he enjoys the benefits of individually appropriate supplementary aids and services, without which he would not be able to benefit from the integrated educational environments and activities he experiences. He lives at home with his mom, dad and sister. He participates in integrated activities with his family in their faith community. He is in a weightlifting class at school with schoolmates who are not disabled. He lifts and works out with them at the local YMCA after school Tuesdays and Saturday mornings. He goes to and from school and to the YMCA in a car pool with his friends. At other times he uses public transportation to travel about his community. Two mornings per week he goes to a bank to learn work skills and how to function in an integrated work setting. He …
>
> He could not enjoy the benefits of these safe and enhancing integrated environments and activities without the extra support of family members, teachers, paraprofessionals, therapists, taxpayers and many others. Chances are great that he, and millions of others within his functioning range, will outlive his parents. When that happens, he still will not be able to survive or thrive by himself. In a socially just society, where will he live? Who will he be with? What will he be doing all day? How much should we spend on him? Indeed, compassionate, humane and supportive actions are wonderful, but there are associated costs. What are some of the options we could actualize for the lowest intellectually functioning individuals within our society?

First, we could kill them and harvest their organs and any other parts of their bodies that others more able might need. Clearly, doing so would lower taxpayer costs. Killing the lowest intellectually functioning one, five, ten or thirty percent of the population would allow even greater cost reductions. However extreme and slippery, there are those who would say, "Let's pick a percent and just do it."

Second, we could require the prenatal testing of all pregnant women and then abort fetuses that have characteristics we do not want. There would be no choice. It would be considered justifiable homicide. It always frustrates and angers us when we experience those who strongly oppose such policies and practices, but also strongly oppose generating tax dollars to help the young survive and thrive after we require or allow them to live. This is compartmentalized social justice.

Third, we could offer no extra taxpayer services. If families or charities cannot pay for what they need to survive or thrive, so be it. If we did so, many would die, tremendous economic, emotional and other burdens would be placed upon aging parents and family members and much of the lives of millions with and without disabilities would be terribly and painfully constricted or wasted. Braddock (2007) reported that in 2000 over 710,000 persons with intellectual disabilities of all ages in the United States were living with caregivers over age 60. In addition, we would have to look at ourselves in mirrors and we would have to explain to our children why we treat people this way.

Fourth, we could regress to earlier times and segregate them in "Handicapped Only" public and private institutions, nursing homes, schools and day activity centers. Indeed, individuals with disabilities are entering homeless shelters, nursing homes or assisted living facilities at a much earlier age and in vastly disproportionate numbers compared with their same age peers (Charlton, 2000). Historically, this option has been extremely costly for taxpayers. For example, in 2002, the average annual cost of confining a person to a state operated institution for individuals with intellectual disabilities in the United States was $135,000. The cost of serving the same person in the home of a family member or in a supported apartment and in supported employment in an integrated community was $20,000 (Rizzo et. al, 2004). Consider the costs of segregating one percent of three hundred million or three million individuals. Also consider the well-documented abuses and wasted lives endemic to segregated settings (Hakim, 2011). No socially just society can tolerate such an option.

Fifth, we could arrange for the lowest intellectually functioning one percent of our population to live, work and play in integrated society. If we held environmental factors constant across individuals, intelligence may not be distributed as is typically depicted by a bell curve, but it would still be distributed unequally. Assume that no matter how it is actually distributed in nature there will always be the highest and lowest intellectually functioning one percents of an inclusive population. Should social justice be distributed unequally as is intelligence? Are there parameters of citizenship that should be available only to certain intellectual portions of the population? We say no, but how intelligence is manifested and supported in the lives of individuals in each grouping might be substantially different. Individuals with significant intellectual disabilities have the same general needs and rights as all others, but they require many different and specific kinds of assistance in education, health care, domestic living, transportation, social relationships, vocational functioning, personal management and other aspects of daily living.

What is compassionate, human and supportive social justice for a thirty year-old man with severe cerebral palsy who is among the lowest intellectually functioning one percent of all citizens in his community? His mother and father have died. He works in the office of an insurance company for less than the local minimum wage for thirty hours per week. A Job Coach paid by taxpayers ensures that he is successful at his work site. He receives medical benefits from the Social Security Administration. He lives in an apartment with another person with disabilities. A Life Coach comes to their apartment several times each week to help with shopping, cleaning, medical activities and cooking. He is involved in aerobics and ceramics at his faith community. He uses public transit and meals on wheels. He and his roommate like movies and go to a theater together about once per week. He …

He does not make enough money to pay all the costs of his apartment and employment assistance, food or other important basic life needs. The county in which he lives gives him tax dollars for that which he cannot pay for himself. What would his life be like if the extra support he receives is taken away?

Many families have fought tirelessly and for many years in order to generate opportunities for their children with significant intellectual and related disabilities to survive and thrive in integrated settings and activities. We now realize that arranging for some to function in integrated settings and activities often result in innovative ways of generating opportunities for others of similar circumstance to do so. New examples of individuals with significant disabilities who lead remarkably productive, safe and rewarding integrated lives surface daily. Thus, we know it can happen and we know how to do it. However, they certainly are part of an extremely small minority. The overwhelming majority of individuals with significant intellectual disabilities are still confined to segregated schools, classes, group homes, nursing homes, shelters and the homes of family members all day as adults.

Sadly, some legislators, union officials, business leaders, parents and a dying breed of professionals are still opposing the fifth option, even though it is the one that will lead us to a socially just society. In short, if compassionate, humane and supportive social justice is being actualized in the lives of a few, we must find ways to expand it to millions of others. Each of us must be able to see, feel, hear or otherwise sense that compassionate, humane and supportive social justice is operational in our lives. The challenge now is bringing that fifth option to scale (Schorr, 1998).

EXTENSION QUESTIONS/ACTIVITIES

1. Brown makes a compelling case for his definition of social justice as compassionate, humane and supportive. His definition emanates from working with students and families with severe disabilities. Do you define and/or contextualize social justice in this manner? Jot down your thoughts and be prepared to share with your colleagues.

2. Check out www.dnai.org website and then click on Chronicle. How as a society that subscribes to liberty and justice for all explain or make sense of "treatment of the unfit" and policies of eugenics? Could the Human

Genome Project support eugenics and is it possible that scientists and politicians could bastardize Brown's definition of social justice?

3. Should social justice be distributed unequally as is intelligence? Take a few minutes to think through this question before answering. Write a heading *Unequal Distribution* on to top of a sheet of paper. Now create one column with the heading *Intelligence* and the other column with the heading *Social Justice*. Jot down how intelligence is distributed unequally in your school i.e., classes for special education students, GATE classes, ELL etc. Notice unequal distribution of social justice (student voice, status, gender, race, class, disability, sexual orientation) at your school and whether there is some overlap with intelligence, especially as it relates to marginalization of groups. Write down your thoughts about social justice within school settings. Now take it one step further and discuss how your thoughts on this topic relate to persons who are vulnerable in our society, in this case, individuals with moderate to severe intellectual disabilities.

REFERENCES

Braddock, D. (2007). Washington rises: Public financial support for intellectual disability in the United States, 1955-2004. *Mental Retardation and Developmental Disabilities Research Reviews, 13*, 169-177.

Brown, L. (1986). Foreword: Then and now. In R. H. Horner, L. H. Meyer, & H. D. B. Fredericks (Eds.), *Education of learners with severe handicaps: Exemplary service strategies* (pp. xi-xiii) Baltimore, MA: Brookes Publishing Co.

Brown, L., Shiraga, B., & Kessler, K. (2006). The quest for ordinary lives: The integrated post-school vocational functioning of 50 workers with significant disabilities. *Research and Practice for Persons with Severe Disabilities, 31*(2), 93-121.

Charlton, J. I. (2000). *Nothing about without us: Disability empowerment and oppression.* Berkeley, CA: University of California Press.

Hakim, D. (2011, March 13). Abused and used: At state-run homes, abuse and impunity. *The New York Times*, pp. A1.

Nussbaum, M. (2006). *Frontiers of justice.* Cambridge, MA: Belknap Press.

Rawls, J. (1999). *Theory of justice: Revised edition.* Cambridge, MA: Belknap Press.

Rizzolo, M. C., Hemp, R., Braddock, D., & Pomeranz-Essley, A. (2004). *The state of the states in development disabilities.* Washington DC: American Association on Mental Retardation.

Schorr, L. (1998). *Common purpose: Strengthening families and neighborhoods to rebuild America.* New York: Anchor Books.

Terzi, L. (2005). Beyond the dilemma of difference: The capability approach to disability and special educational needs. *Journal of Educational Philosophy, 39*(3), 443-459.

Walker, M. (2006). Towards a capability-based theory of social justice for education policymaking. *Journal of Education Policy, 21*(2), 163-185.

Lou Brown
University of Wisconsin

PATRICIA A. WHANG

SECTION 3: INTRODUCTION

The Ties That Bind

The touchstone that coalesces insights from the third set of essays has to do with the importance of recognizing the interconnected, endlessly interwoven, and relational nature of all aspects of life (Hanh, 1988; Salzberg, 2003). A lack of awareness or consideration of connections or interdependence distorts our understanding of reality; thus potentially sustaining and nurturing the status quo. If I am unaware of or feel no need to consider the ramification of my choices through the web of interconnections then it is likely that, for example, practices that harm the environment or oppress people will be allowed to continue undetected and unchallenged. Inaccurate, partial, or missing perceptions of reality impact the quality of choices that are made, which again, because of the endlessly interwoven nature of life has ripple effects that remain largely unperceived. For example, without intentionally seeking to understand the inputs required in the production of this piece of paper, I have no awareness of whether or not it has been produced in a way that is sustainable or damaging to the earth, or whether people involved in the production of this sheet of paper earn a living wage or work in safe conditions.

The ability to see the truth of interconnectedness has been referred to as "right view" in Buddhist teachings (Salzberg, 2003). Such a view is important to an understanding of social justice because it allows for the cultivation of a mind-state referred to as loving-kindness, which commits one to being an ally of all beings. Cultivating this mind-state is necessary because, as Cornel West (n.d.) explains, "… since justice is what love looks like in public, you can't talk about loving folk and not fighting for justice." Loving-kindness should not be understood as a feeling, sentiment, or manufactured emotion, but rather a view or "… an essential way of seeing that arises when we free ourselves from our normal mental habits that create division and boundaries and barriers, that create a sense of self and other" (Salzberg, 2003, In teaching loving-kindness).

Being an ally of all beings requires empathy and compassion and the recognition that one's liberation is intertwined with the liberation of all beings. Taking this notion of interdependence and interconnectedness seriously wobbles perceptions that we are different than, separate from, and/or independent of others and thus necessitates abandoning operating from an egocentric or self-absorbed perspective (Chodron, 2008). An emphasis on differences and separateness serves to perpetuate the status quo, especially given that societal social stratification is hierarchical organized, so that groups differ in terms of their status, privilege, and freedom and

Louis G. Denti and Patricia A. Whang (eds.), Rattling Chains: Exploring Social Justice in Education, 87–89.
© 2012 *Sense Publishers. All rights reserved.*

view one another as adversaries who are continually working to keep what they have or acquire what others have. If I perceive you to be different from me, then I am less likely to join forces with you and mobilize our power in numbers to demand change. Perhaps this is why we are socialized to be ignorant of and/or unconcerned about connections and interrelations. For example, Nurenberg (2011) points out that the privileged white suburban students that he teaches do not feel a sense of connection to the oppressed and thus lack outrage at prevailing social conditions. So, in his teaching experiences they do not buy-in to the need for social justice education. Nurenberg (2011) suggests that for such students, it may be necessary to "create touch points of potential empathy and identification with those who suffer race- and class-based oppression" (p. 54).

With respect to superficial or non-existent connections between people, the Dalai Lama points out that our dependence on others has weakened because of our heavy reliance on machines and services (Lama, 2001). This has the effect of creating the impression that others are not important to our happiness and vice versa, the happiness of others is independent of our happiness. According to Hopkins (2001), misperceptions – or wrong views - also occur because we mainly encounter others through the medium of sight. That is, "we mainly *see* other people, but we mainly *feel* ourselves and remain primarily concerned with our own feelings of warmth, cold, hunger, thirst, breathing, having this please or that pain. We use radically different modes for self and other" (p. 31). Reliance on sight results in superficial knowledge about others based on factors like differences in skin color or body shape. Being in touch with our feelings keeps alive our desire to attain happiness and avoid suffering. Our superficial perceptions of other people may stunt our ability to find common ground with others based on their similar desires to attain happiness and avoid suffering. Finding common ground with others is essential, because "understanding that we all want happiness and don't' want suffering is the basis for love, compassion, kindness" (Hopkins, 2001). And as Cornel West (n.d.) so poetically reminds us, "justice is love on legs, spilling over into the public sphere." To reinforce this section's touchstone, each of the titles for the essays in this section contain the phrase "Kindness is Society." This is to serve as a reminder, that as the Dalai Lama points out, "it's impossible to have society without concern for other people" (Hopkins, 2001, p. 29).

The first essay in this section is *Diane Ravitch's*, who underscores the importance of developing a critical understanding of the interconnections between schools and society, as well as interrogating the assumption that schools should be expected to fix societal ills (e.g., drug abuse, gangs, childhood obesity). Not acknowledging interconnections is said to preserve the status quo, by diverting attention away from significant factors such as poverty, which eradication of requires sacrifices to be made by the elite. The piece by *Etta R. Hollins* explores social justice from individual, collective, and political/social movement perspectives. Also, the author reminds us that social justice movements are inherently a recognition of the interconnection or intertwined nature of lives and the need to actively work together to pursue greater access, equity, and dignity. Next, *Aydin Bal* builds on these insights through stories based on personal and professional experiences. Furthermore he articulates the need for, what he terms a participatory social justice, because of the interconnected nature of lives. *Gilbert R. Guerin and Louis G. Denti* examine why injustice persists in the face of known causes and effective solutions. Drawing from the vast literature on dropouts the authors make us aware that a lot is known about predicting who is going to drop out. This brings to mind the question, who is benefitting from the status quo? Clearly it is neither the individuals who drop out, nor society. Next, *Wayne Sailor and Nikki Wolf* make broad connections between some of this nation's founding ideals and a consideration of how contradictions inherent in those ideals impact people. As the authors point out, aspirations to make good on this country's democratic ideals are complicated by our commitments to capitalism. Sailor and Wolf use the example of charter schools to illuminate how the privatization of what has traditionally been a publically entrusted entity can serve as a disincentive to work toward a more socially just society. Furthermore, their example illustrates how the drive for profit making can serve to divide citizens from one another.

REFERENCES

Chödrön, P. (2008). Shambhala Sun – Turn your thinking upside down. *Shambhala Sun.* Magazine. Retrieved July 30, 2012, from http://www.shambhalasun.com/index.php?option=com_content& task=view&id=3087&Itemid=0.

Cornel West's Catastrophic Love | Cornel West | Big Think. (n.d.). Retrieved August 1, 2011, from http://bigthink.com/ideas/17240.

Hanh, T. N. (1988). *The heart of understanding: Commentaries on the Prajnaparamita Heart Sutra.* (P. Levitt, Ed.). Parallax Press.

Hopkins, J. (2001). *Cultivating compassion: A Buddhist perspective* (1st ed.). Broadway.

Lama, T. D. (2001). *Ethics for the new millennium.* Riverhead Trade.

Nurenberg, D. (2011). What does injustice have to do with me? A pedagogy of the privileged. *Harvard Educational Review, 81*(1), 50-63.

Salzberg, S. (2003, January). Becoming the ally of all beings. *Shambhala Sun.* Retrieved from http://www.shambhalasun.com/index.php?option=com_content&task=view&id=1630&Itemid=0.

DIANE RAVITCH

KINDNESS IS SOCIETY: THE PLIGHT AND PROMISE OF SOCIAL JUSTICE IN PUBLIC EDUCATION

Diane Ravitch, one of America's foremost educational historians responds to a series of questions about social justice and public education posited by the co-editors of this book. Dr. Ravitch is known for her insightful commentary based on years of battling for teachers whether on the right or left of the argument.

"What is social justice" and "why is or is it not important to you?"

I would define social justice as fairness. With reference to education, the issue would be 'do children have equal opportunity to get a good education?' It is important to me because one of the basic premises of our society is equal justice for all, meaning fairness for all, in both a legal sense and with reference to education. I don't think we have fairness now, but the struggle for fairness, for equal justice, is one that we must wage again and again, particularly because our economy continues to generate unequal opportunity, as income inequality grows, jobs are outsourced, and many states are cutting the funding for education and social services. So long as there is unequal opportunity, so long as some have far greater advantage than others, the struggle for social justice must continue. No society has achieved it, ever, and we validate our own humanity by continuing to insist on changes that improve the lives of others.

How has your definition of social justice shifted and evolved in particular historical moments or with changing contextual factors (e.g., current policies)?

As I explain in my recent book, *Death and Life of the Great American School System: How Testing and Choice Are Undermining Education*, I spent many years believing that schools could solve many of our most important social problems and that they were failing to do so. I supported choice and accountability on the assumption or hope that they would provide wider opportunity for children who live in poverty and for minorities who are often at a disadvantage in education. Although I was immersed in some of the leading conservative think tanks in the nation for many years, I began to change my mind as I watched these policies come to fruition. I saw charter schools turn into vehicles for privatization, not collaborating with public education but seeking to compete with it, often to the benefit of for-profit entrepreneurs. I saw accountability turn into a regime of testing and punishment that did nothing to help children but quite a lot to label them, their

Louis G. Denti and Patricia A. Whang (eds.), Rattling Chains: Exploring Social Justice in Education, 91–94.
© 2012 *Sense Publishers. All rights reserved.*

teachers, and their schools, as failures (setting the stage for privatization). I recognized, returning to themes I had written about in the past, that schools are inextricably intertwined with society, that schools reflect society, and that schools alone cannot change society. I also became very upset by the environment of attacking teachers and schools for society's injustices, while ignoring the sources of injustice (poverty and racial isolation).

Why or why not fight for more socially just schools and is it possible to achieve both equity and excellence in American schools?

The schools are a primary mechanism for fighting injustice. They are for many kids the best chance they have to improve their lives. But schools alone cannot right the wrongs of society. Today, the gravest threat to social justice is the fact that so many political and business leaders have decided that schools alone can bring about "educational equity," especially if they do more testing and if there are more privately managed charter schools. This agenda conveniently takes off the table any discussions of poverty. It does so explicitly. We hear that "education is the civil rights issue of our time," and "poverty is just an excuse" for low achievement, and schools alone can bring about the just world and equity we seek. All of this is a smokescreen for more testing and more charter schools because those promoting this line do not suggest that society should pay more for education or tax billionaires or provide a wider range of medical and social services for those who need them. In the summer of 2010, civil rights groups issued a framework in which they specifically complained that the Obama administration says, "education is the civil rights issue of our time" yet promote competition for federal funding among the states. States don't have civil rights, said the groups, individuals do, and the administration's Race to the Top sent federal money to only 11 states and the District of Columbia. To erode the principle that federal funding is based on need, on equity, is to abandon a very important principle of social justice. To promote competition for federal funding among states and districts will leave many children with less money for their education. But what is especially obnoxious is to see the current "education reform" movement led by Wall Street hedge fund managers, entrepreneurs, and others who see education as an investment opportunity.

What would you consider to be an example of effective social justice work in American education today?

The daily work of millions of our nation's teachers, which today is unrecognized, unrewarded, and unpraised. I admire the concept of the Harlem Children's Zone, but I don't admire the way it has been taken up by publicists to argue against public education and to advocate for privatization of education.

How would or would it not impact schools if the general public/politicians/ academics embraced or worked from a commitment to social justice?

If we were to look at education from the perspective of social justice, we would look at schools in relation to society. We would see the ways in which schools might collaborate with social service agencies and community organizations to strengthen the supports for children, in terms of medical care, nutrition, and a social network of caring adults. But we would go beyond the immediate school to look at policies to reduce poverty, to improve housing, to make economic opportunity more widely available, and to make sure that children grow up in healthy and supportive settings. We would, above all, dedicate ourselves to reducing the appalling child poverty rates, which now are about 20% (and rising) possibly the highest of all industrial or post-industrial nations. We compare ourselves on educational tests to nations in Europe and Asia where the child poverty rate is less than 10% or even less than 5%, and we pretend that it doesn't matter that so many children grow up in desperate circumstances. So many of those who now talk about equality and talk about "education is the civil rights issue of our time" are determined to say that poverty doesn't matter. It does matter. So long as the issue of poverty is off the table, as so many leaders demand, we will not address the root causes of social injustice. Many of those who now blame the schools for all the ills of society are unwilling to support better funding for schools or medical care or social services. In effect, what they argue is that privatization and testing are a sure route to equality and social justice, even though these strategies advance stratification, not equality.

EXTENSION QUESTIONS/ACTIVITIES

1. Ravitch's answer to the question what is social justice and why is or is it not important to you generated a particularly provocative comment for those committed to social justice work. Does Ravitch suggest that as long as we are, structurally, a capitalist society, that the struggle for equal justice will go on and perhaps ultimately be ineffective? More specifically, does she also suggest that commitments to social justice may ultimately be a useful distraction to keep those with a - to use Friere's term - critical consciousness - engaged in ultimately futile activities? Write down your response and be prepared to discuss your thoughts with colleagues or classmates.

2. How can one be assured that framing the issue as one of poverty is not contributing another smokescreen as essentially obfuscating the need for more money for education and providing medical and social services? Perhaps it can be argued that we've waged a "war on poverty" and James Comer's work connecting schools to social and medical services has existed for a long time. So, could it be that the root cause is more about those putting up the smokescreen(s) and that they are trying to protect (power, privilege, their pocketbooks?) by distracting us? A thoughtful response including checking out information regarding the war on poverty and James Comer's work is in order.

3. Check out Diane Ravitch's website www.dianeravitch.com and find one or two compelling past or current ideas that resonate for you. Jot down your thoughts and be prepared to have a discussion either with a partner or in a small group.

REFERENCES

Ravitch, D. (2010). *The death and life of the great American school system: How testing and choices are undermining education.* New York: Basic Books.

Diane Ravitch
New York University

ETTA R. HOLLINS

KINDNESS IS SOCIETY: THE INDIVIDUAL AND COLLECTIVE ESSENCE OF SOCIAL JUSTICE

Social justice is a moral position, a philosophical stance, and a social/political movement with multiple dimensions based on the core values that support the highest quality in human life conditions and experiences for all people; where people live together in harmony, with opportunities for full participation in the society; where all contributions are encouraged and appreciated, with freedom from oppression and systematic subordination of members of one group to another; and with access to the collective benefits and resources of the society that enrich and make life meaningful for everyone. In a social justice moral stance the highest value is placed on ethical standards of commitment, integrity, responsibility, and trustworthiness. In a social justice philosophical stance, the highest value is placed on the protection of human rights, caring about and for others in the society, supporting the maximum potential for human growth and development, civic and social engagement and responsibility, and the pursuit of excellence in all endeavors. Engaging social justice as a social/political movement means taking particular individual and collective actions to ensure that the moral and philosophical dimensions are accomplished and maintained.

A social justice moral position sets the standards of commitment, integrity, responsibility, and trustworthiness for engagement when carrying out the core values in the philosophical stance. The system of beliefs and understandings that form the basis of the philosophical stance is reflected in the consistency in particular perspectives, practices, behaviors, and actions aimed at enriching public spaces such as governance, public policy, and public schooling that serve the common good. For example, central to the social justice philosophical stance is the belief that all citizens should be equally protected and served by governance and public policies, and provided equal access to high quality public schooling and meaningful opportunities for learning. The basic benefits, privileges, and responsibilities of citizenship should not be proportioned on the basis of power, privilege, race, or social status. Further, those who attain power and status in the society should exercise caution to avoid exploitation or further disempowerment of those with less power and status.

The imbalance in power and status in the society, and the inequitable treatment of those with less power and status is the focus of social justice. While social justice is a multidimensional concept with a wide range of perspectives, the common focus is on access, equity, and human dignity. Individuals and groups converge on this single focus through collective action from multiple perspectives.

Louis G. Denti and Patricia A. Whang (eds.), Rattling Chains: Exploring Social Justice in Education, 95–98.
© 2012 *Sense Publishers. All rights reserved.*

For example, some individuals and groups focus on policies and practices that privilege some and disempower others such as environmental pollution in low-income neighborhoods; others focus on access to the best education and health practices, or gay rights. Individuals and groups have different reasons for their focus on social justice that may be economic, political, psychological, or social. These different perspectives are applied in different settings within agencies and institutions, social organizations, and educational settings through promoting changes in awareness, policies, and practices. These different approaches and perspectives tend to share a single focus on access, equity, and human dignity.

The focus on access, equity and human dignity when addressed in a single institution can take many different perspectives and approaches. For example, when social justice is applied to public education it can address the purpose of schooling, access to high quality teaching and opportunities for learning, as well as how the curriculum is framed and issues of gender, race, ethnicity, and differences in cognitive and physical challenges. The framing of the curriculum is in itself a complex and, at times, a controversial issue. The framing of the curriculum and the pedagogical approach are at the heart of the purpose of schooling. This is apparent in Moje's (2007) distinction between socially just pedagogy and social justice pedagogy. Socially just pedagogy is described as ensuring that all youth have equitable opportunities for learning mainstream knowledge and academic literacy practices as preparation for economic and social success; however, this does not ameliorate the existing system of cultural and political dominance. In contrast, social justice pedagogy, in addition to providing equitable opportunities for learning mainstream knowledge and academic literacy practices, provides for transformative knowledge and transformation of the learner and the society through opportunities to question, challenge, and reconstruct knowledge for the purpose of creating a more just society.

The existing system of cultural and political dominance denies equitable access to learning for students of color and low-income students, especially African American and Latino students in urban schools. These students tend to be taught by teachers with less preparation and experience, with higher teacher turnover rates, and higher rates of daily absences; and are less likely to have access to a rigorous curriculum and the best pedagogical practices. Yet, on standardized tests and college entrance examinations students of color and low-income students are expected to compete with their mainstream peers who had the advantages of highly qualified and experienced teachers, a rigorous curriculum, and the best pedagogical practices. Recent efforts to address the issue of equity in school learning including the No Child Left Behind Act of 2001 and, more recently, the Race to the Top have had little impact on school and classroom practices.

However, an emerging line of research indicates that in situations where teachers subscribe to the values of social justice including ethical standards of commitment, integrity, responsibility, and trustworthiness they are better prepared to support learning for traditionally underserved students. For example, Wilson, Corbett, and Williams (2000) reported on a teacher community at an urban junior high school where teachers collectively *assumed responsibility* for ensuring that students reached the desired level of performance by adapting instruction to the students' needs and incorporating their prior knowledge and experiences, re-teaching concepts that students did not understand, and when something did not seem to be working for a student, the team of teachers met with the student and the student's parents to develop a new approach for the student. The day was structured to support students' academic performance. The last session of the day was devoted to re-teaching and enrichment. This was when students who needed help received it from their regular teachers and those who had achieved mastery could work on extensions that would allow them to earn a higher grade. In this collaborative context teachers were committed to maintaining high academic standards for their students and for collectively supporting students' in achieving the expected learning outcomes. These teachers developed a social context based on integrity and trustworthiness among and between teachers and students.

There are related narrative accounts of situations in low performing urban schools where teachers do not assume responsibility for ensuring that students achieve the desired learning outcomes or make efforts to develop a social context based on integrity and trust among and between teachers and students. These teachers do not subscribe to the values, perspectives, or practices of a social justice philosophical stance. The prevailing ideology in the teacher community is based on a negative deficit perspective on the students, rather than one focused on a vision of their students becoming well-educated individuals making valued contributions to the society. In these situations, the teachers' negative deficit ideology maintains and reinforces teaching practices that result in low academic performance. For example, Sipe (2004) presented an account of the social context in a dysfunctional low-performing middle school where teachers had little respect for their students and frequently engaged in an exchange of name calling that included language laced with expletives. The teachers in this situation did not feel obligation or responsibility for working to improve the situation. Sipe perceives four options: "1) you cope by falling prey to the inhumanity of the 'us vs. them' mentality and act accordingly; 2) you insulate yourself by refusing to care and bide your time until you can transfer or retire; or 3) the stress gets to you and your mental health suffers" (p. 336). The fourth option was to try to change the school from the classroom, but Sipe believed the option of leaving the school at the end of his two-year commitment for a position in a better school was the preferred choice. Changing this situation would require transforming the prevailing ideology and teachers' attitudes towards their responsibility for ensuring that students meet high academic standards and for developing a social context based on integrity and trustworthiness among and between teachers and students.

Ultimately, social justice as it relates to the education of underserved and underrepresented groups requires activism and advocacy – a social and political human rights movement aimed at protecting the rights of presently underserved students to a high quality education in the nation's public schools. This means bringing into all public school settings administrators and teachers who subscribe to high ethical standards of commitment, integrity, responsibility, and trustworthiness; and, who place the highest value on the protection of human rights, supporting the maximum potential for human growth and development, accepting personal responsibility for the outcomes of one's own professional practice, and working collaboratively with others in the pursuit of excellence in all endeavors. This will ensure that all students have access to high quality public education. This is the essence of social justice in school practices.

EXTENSION QUESTIONS/ACTIVITIES

1. Hollins talks about a moral and philosophical stance that undergirds social justice. From your point of view, what ways does or doesn't a philosophical and moral stance support social justice?

2. Hollins asserts that, "The existing system of cultural and political dominance denies equitable access to learning for students of color and low-income students, especially African American and Latino students in urban schools." She goes on to explain her assertion. Do you agree or disagree with her assertion? Write down your point of view, and then in pairs or in a small group, discuss your thoughts with your colleagues.

3. Many schools have mottos written that subscribe to ethical standards of commitment, integrity, responsibility, and trustworthiness, yet spend little time in ensuring they are understood by faculty, staff, and students as well as taught. If your school or agency has developed ethical standards, how are they incorporated into the fabric of the schools/agency culture? If your ethical standards appear to be window dressing, why do you think that is so and what could be done to change that phenomenon?

REFERENCES

Ellis, C., & Smith, S. D. (2005). *Say it plain: A century of great African American speeches.* New York: W. W. Norton & Company.

Moje, E. B. (2007). Chapter 1, Developing socially just subject-matter instruction: A review of the literature on disciplinary literacy teaching. *Review of Research in Education, 31*, 1-44.

Sipe, R. (2004). Voices inside schools: Newjack-Teaching in a failing middle school. *Harvard Educational Review, 74*(3), 330-339.

VanSledright, B. (2008). Narratives of nation-state, historical knowledge, and school history education. *Review of Research in Education, 32*, 109-146.

Wilson, B., Corbett, D., & Williams, B. (2000). *A discussion on school reform – Case 1: All students learning at Granite Junior High.* Teachers College Record, Retrieved October 30, 2000, from http:www.tcrecord.org, ID 10619.

Etta R. Hollins
University of Missouri-Kansas City

AYDIN BAL

KINDNESS IS SOCIETY: PARTICIPATORY SOCIAL JUSTICE FOR ALL

In the second meeting of a graduate seminar on culture and disability, a PhD student shared his reflections over the readings of the week. It soon became obvious that he had not read the assigned readings. He was sharing his reflections about the topic of the week, under- and over-representation of racial minority students in special education programs (i.e., disproportionality). Almost instantly the student drew a direct causal link between minority students' background and the higher levels of risk for academic failure and disabilities. His argument was all too familiar. It started from minority parents' lack of care and resources for their children's education, their inadequacy in providing role models, aspirations, and educational opportunities and ended with the cultural deprivation.

In the end of his ten-minute reflections, the student reached a clear conclusion that minority students' culture, the culture of poverty, caused disproportionality. He did not even have the smallest doubt that the selected readings from prominent special education scholars would contradict what he assumed those readings were about (i.e., academic and behavioral risk factors that minority students bring to schools). The student caught up with the readings in the following weeks. And he was on a quest for developing more comprehensive conceptualization of those issues moving beyond overly deterministic deficit-based views. However, I kept thinking about that incident. How could a doctoral student of special education who came from a low-income rural family in an economically developing country and experienced discrimination as a Muslim immigrant in the US so easily make such an argument that blamed minority students and families for educational outcome disparities?

I am an assistant professor preparing future special education teachers and researchers. I have worked with non-dominant students based on race, language, and class and immigrant/refugee youth experiencing behavioral difficulties and psychological disorders in urban schools and juvenile justice system. My research includes understanding and addressing complex and enduring equity issues such as outcome and opportunity disparities. I aim at developing culturally responsive behavioral intervention models to address those disparities through the formation of positive, supportive, and inclusive school cultures. The argument my student made in the seminar summed up the messages that I have received during my education and professional work as a psychologist and special educator both in my home country, Turkey, and in the US. Yet it is still surprising to see the extent to which educators can automatically equate cultural, linguistic and ability differences

Louis G. Denti and Patricia A. Whang (eds.), Rattling Chains: Exploring Social Justice in Education, 99–109.
© 2012 *Sense Publishers. All rights reserved.*

with deficits and how non-dominant families' cultural practices as risk factors has been and still is the default mode nationally and internationally as seemingly scientific and bias-free explanations.

In this chapter, I explore the intersection of race, social class, and ability to discuss prominence of the deficit-perspectives. I argue for a participatory social justice theory, as an alternative analytical and applied model to address the outcome disparities and to design better educational contexts for *all* students.

INTERSECTION OF RACE, CLASS, AND ABILITY

In the US education system race and social class have been interlocked in complex ways to maintain lasting negative educational and socioeconomic outcomes for racial minority youth from low income-families such as lower academic achievement and higher drop out rates (Darling-Hammond, 2010). Moreover, if we look at the intersection of race, class, and ability, we see that those disparities are exaggerated for non-dominant students. Minority students (e.g., African-American, Native-American, and Latino) are overrepresented in special education for more subjective- high incidence- disability categories such as behavioral disorders or learning disabilities that are made up of almost 70% of all students in special education. Once in special education, minority students are placed in more restrictive settings and have lower post secondary outcomes compared to their peers (Losen & Orfiled, 2002). They are also disproportionally subjected to exclusionary school discipline and severe punishments such as mechanical restraints (e.g. being strapped down) (Civil Rights Data Collection, 2012).

The deficit-oriented perspectives explaining those disparities by individual risk factors associated with non-dominant cultural practices and environments are sunk into the social psyche of our society. For example, students from privileged racial, social, and economic backgrounds who benefited from unequally distributed educational opportunities throughout their lives explained their success with their hard work, higher motivation and intelligence (Kozol, 2005). They did not acknowledge the structural and social opportunities such as highly trained teachers, positive, safe, and academically rich school climates, challenging curriculum, high expectations, extra curricular activities, and valued social and cultural capital, which they and their families have unequally benefited from generation after generation. Privileged students may perceive that schools provide a fair opportunity in which they become more successful because they have superior moral and intellectual qualities.

Moreover, deficit-views dominated the teacher education programs and educational research. Being white and coming from middle and high-income levels have become the norms against which anyone or any cultural groups are represented as missing moral, psychological or social qualities. A random search of an introductory level special education textbook can attest to this point. In those textbooks, culture is associated only with minority people and their difference becomes more visible. Usually there is one chapter about cultural and linguistic diversity. In the rest of the textbook one finds theories of learning, development, or ability and instructional practices as if the information is culture-blind and universal. The diversity chapter usually mentions minority students' and families' different values (e.g., collectivism) and characteristics (e.g., learning styles, eye contact) in an essentialist way. It also includes the information about outcome disparities and how you may work with non-dominant families in "culturally responsive ways" so that the non-dominant families and students can cooperate with the school expectations and practices. Our schools and teaching/learning practices are already culturally responsive toward views and practices of dominant cultural groups who are white, middle class, protestant, heterosexual, and without disability (Banks & Banks, 2007). This has important implications in the lives of non-dominant students. Non-dominant students' ways of knowing, behaving, and being are often devalued, so that for example, academic identities of racial minority students may be constructed as disruptive, resistant, outcast, and unlikely to succeed in schools (Wortham, 2006). Another important implication of the deficit-perspectives for non-dominant students is that they can also internalize the dominant value system of the school that marginalize them and see themselves and others from non-dominant backgrounds through the social mirror of the dominant group as evinced by my student's comments in the seminar. Without a critical examination, educators from non-dominant racial and linguistic groups and social class can very well engage in practices and theories that are inept to understand complex life experiences, perspectives, and strengths of non-dominant students and communities.

As students, families, schools, and communities embrace the waves of diversity that surge through our schools, future practitioners and researchers need to develop a critical social justice perspective through which cultural, linguistics, and ability differences are not just valued but also used as resources for forming more effective learning contexts for *all* students.

FROM DEFICITS TO STRENGTHS – RISKS TO RESILIENCY

My personal and professional experience in non-dominant communities helped me to see the role of critical social justice theory as a means to understand and address lasting outcome and opportunity gaps that those communities experience. I grew up in a low-income working class family. Both of my parents had severe orthopedic disabilities. Each had more than ten orthopedic surgeries due to gradually declining physical capabilities and accumulated effects of physical disabilities. They did not have a formal education and were illiterate. By the age of eighteen, my family had moved for more than thirty times between houses and cities. Moreover, my parents belong to a religious minority group that has been politically and economically marginalized and subjected to social violence and discriminatory practices for centuries. In short, from the conventional perspective, I was a living embodiment of the "at risk" student category for academic failure.

In Turkey, an economically developing country, being poor was hard. But having a disability, being illiterate, and coming from a non-dominant marginalized group interactively made my family's life harder based on how Turkish society and government are organized. Almost all of the instances in my memory about my parents being disabled, illiterate or poor involve other people in a social event. Those events can be as ordinary for my parents as taking a daily bus trip to work, or attending a parent-teacher meeting, or asking for services that were officially designated as their rights such as physical accommodations. In such instances where I remembered feeling my parents were disabled, those aspects of their/our life were used to degrade them, insult them, or exclude them because of how they looked, talked, or acted or what they demanded as their rights. I do not remember my parents as being incapable in any physical or social tasks or in a gathering with family or friends but in a social or bureaucratic event where the others made the differences that my parents and our family had more visible and where my parents were asked to be invisible and silent. Depending on the situation or what is at stake (my education or their employment), my parents complied with what the others or the situation dictated and acted in such ways. But in other instances, they resisted how they were positioned negatively or excluded from certain social activities. In those instances, they eventually got either what their rights were in the first place (respect, power, status, or a voice) or punished and further marginalized. In short, their life, struggles, needs, strengths, and achievements could not be understood only by focusing on what they individually could or could not do but as situated in enabling or disabling cultural-historical contexts where individual, institutional, and social factors are collectively negotiated and orchestrated by my parents and the others as they try to reach their goals.

In the majority of my adult life, I have worked with youth from historically marginalized communities who were experiencing social and behavioral difficulties in and outside of schools. My professional training in special education and clinical psychology demanded me to identify as efficiently as possible what is "special" about a child's mind and/or behaviors. I was being trained to look for what is wrong with/in a child. However, my first-hand experience showed the possibilities of understanding educational and psychosocial difficulties that children experience in relation to their interactions with other people in schools in which the children find themselves. During my graduate program, I volunteered in social justice organizations such as the Amnesty International and worked with refugee families in their resettlement. Specifically working with a group of refugee youth, Lost Boys and Girls of Sudan, opened up my mind about the complexity of voices, experiences, and strengths in non-dominant students and communities. Young members of the Dinka, Nuer and other indigenous tribes of Southern Sudan who called themselves the Lost Boys and Girls became child casualties of the world's longest-running civil war. In the mid-1980s government troops from Northern Sudan attacked their villages. Thousands of children, many less than seven years old at that time, saw their families killed and their villages destroyed. As their villages were attacked, these young children ran away leaving behind the security of their village life, adult guidance and the love of family. Approximately

30,000 war orphans began a journey that took them more than a thousand miles through three countries in search of safety. More than half of these children died from starvation, disease, and attacks by wild animals and government militia. Those who survived ultimately reached the Kakuma refugee camp in Kenya where they spent the next ten years. In 2001, nearly 4,000 Lost Boys and 89 Lost Girls came to the US in what became the nation's largest resettlement of unaccompanied minor refugees.

The Lost Boys Center asked me to develop an educational and behavioral health program as the Lost Boys and Girls were increasingly struggling with psychological and educational problems, substance abuse, and involvement in criminal justice system. In the beginning, whenever I interacted with them, as a well-trained special educator and psychologist, I was constantly looking for trauma-related symptoms such as emotional numbness, hopelessness about the future or memory problems and possible effects of those symptoms in their activities that I thought determined social and educational problems they experience in the US. As I gained a better understanding of their individual and collective histories, I realized that their lives and struggles were way too complex and could not be captured through individual manifestations of traumatic stress reactions. Under extremely harsh circumstances they have found innovative ways to use physical and social resources around them; formed a transnational social support network and took care of each other and their extended families. They had to adapt to ever changing physical and social contexts and mastered survival skills such as defending themselves against soldiers, militia, wild animals, famine (e.g., eating wet mud to survive), building shacks and running small businesses selling cigarettes or other goods to adults who lived in the Kakuma refugee camp. In the US, the Lost Boys and Girls have engaged in political activism for the independence of South Sudan, raised public awareness toward the human rights violations in Sudan, and created bridges between people of South Sudan and governmental and non-governmental organizations in the US.

Yes, their refuge experience was traumatic and some were dealing with psychological, educational, and social problems that were real and disabling. But those problems were not free from the social, political, and economic conditions that they found in the US, a highly stratified society along the lines of race and class. The Lost Boys and Girls were placed in inner-city neighborhoods. Those impoverished and highly segregated urban neighborhoods offered extremely toxic living environments for its non-dominant residents, racial minority families as well as the newly arrived immigrants/refugees (Anyon, 2005). For example, the more time immigrant/refugee youth spend in the US, the worse socio-economic, educational, and physical health-related issues they encounter (e.g., obesity, cardiovascular issues, or substance abuse) (Suarez-Orozco, Rhodes, & Milburn, 2009). As African refugees, they faced social and institutional prejudices. Soda cans and racial slurs were thrown at them as they walked on the street. Their interactions with police and the legal system were always challenging because of their collective negative history with people in uniform, their inexperience in the workings of the US legal system, and institutionalized racism. Several of them had jail time due to some minor offenses (traffic violations) and dealt with police brutality. They did not have access to any proper health care for mental and physical health issues resulted from living as refugees or child soldiers (e.g., missing limps, traumatic brain injury). The US government did not provide an adequate financial, social, health-care, and educational support program that could help this refugee group and the practitioners (teachers, social workers, and police) who worked with them. In schools, they were identified with speech and language disabilities or social skills problems in schools without any acknowledgement to social and structural challenges they found in the US as African refugees even though each could speak 3-4 languages, lived in more than four countries and adapted to diverse cultural communities in those countries. On the other hand, a majority of the Lost Boys and Girls were doing well working 2-3 low paying jobs, looking after their families in the US and Africa, and putting themselves through technical colleges or universities. How could I, as a practitioner, explain Lost Boys' and Girls' struggles solely based on individual symptoms of PTSD and design a support program without considering their social agency, resilience, and the historical, structural and sociocultural contexts, which those refugee youth found themselves in?

In what follows, I describe a participatory social justice perspective that I have appropriated based on my personal and professional experience. It focuses on outcome and opportunity disparities on the ground of differences in race, ability, and class but it goes beyond that: Participatory social justice perspective honors the complexity and diversity in the lives of non-dominant students and explores the sociocultural and institutional processes that reproduce and maintain those outcome disparities and socially unjust spaces where non-dominant youth and families are excluded or positioned through deficit-models.

BEYOND OUTCOME DISPARITIES: PARTICIPATORY SOCIAL JUSTICE FOR ALL

The most common definition of social justice is based on the idea of distributional equality. A *fair* distribution of goods and resources such as food, health care, education, and other social services among all people, specifically for the benefit of the weakest members of the society is the main concern (Rawls, 1999). This is definitely vital to focus on the surface of inequalities. However, with this distributive justice perspective, the structural and institutional processes such as the racialization of ability or systemic exclusion of minority students and families, which produce inequalities in the first place, are not challenged.

The outcome-oriented distributive justice sees policy level changes and educational reforms as solutions to inequalities. Such initiatives include racial desegregation and inclusion of people with disabilities ordering the *de jure* integration of public schools on the basis of separate is not equal. Those top-to-bottom initiatives are essential and necessary for addressing social injustice. But they are not enough since policies often ignore the unfairness of the processes. If we stay at the outcome level and hope the fair policies will solve social and educational inequalities in our society, we may face a danger of making the unjust processes reproducing those outcome disparities invisible and further reinforce the deficit-oriented perspectives toward minority families because of continuing negative outcomes that non-dominant youth with disabilities experience even after those changes were enacted. Racial desegregation in schools was, for example, a morally right and socially just action. However, both in terms of the immediate and long-term results of racial desegregation, racially non-dominant students and communities were negatively affected. In the more immediate term, formerly all black schools were closed, students were moved into all white schools with better facilities, and African-American teachers, administrators, and families lost their status and influence over the education of their children. African-American students in the newly desegregated schools were disproportionally placed in segregated remedial education programs for more subjectively identified disability categories such as mild mental retardation within the "inclusive" schools. In the long-term, today schools are more segregated than they were 50 years ago. As Kozol (2005) points out a majority of racial minority students were educated in majority-minority urban school districts that are not properly equipped for providing high quality educational opportunities. Likewise, the enactment of federal law P. L. 94-142, The Education for All Handicapped Children Act of 1975 was implemented to address discrimination and social outcome disparities against people with disabilities whose right to access equal educational opportunities had been historically denied. While this was an important achievement, special education has not produced intended academic and social outcomes for minority students placed in special education. Special education placement that is meant to allocate appropriate services and additional resources for children with disabilities may also stigmatize students, segregate them from their peers, expose them to low expectations and a weak curriculum, and limit post-school outcomes such as employment options, income level, access to higher education, and life satisfaction (Losen & Orfield, 2002).

Social justice is not an abstract notion of being fair or something "handed down" by educational reforms, it is a shared responsibility of people in the socially unjust systems they inhabit and reproduce (Soja, 2010). Social justice is not a static state, the ultimate fairness, but a continuous collective struggle. In other words, whatever we do or do not do in our daily lives has real implications in the lives of the others who posit less power since our actions can either challenge or reproduce socially unjust processes that starts from our lives. Therefore, I propose that participatory social justice as an alternative to distributive justice can challenge educational inequalities such as racial learning opportunities gap or disproportionality. Participatory social justice encompasses two simultaneous actions: Critically exploring outcome and opportunity disparities as well as exploring and working against the sociopolitical and educational processes producing and maintaining those long-lasting outcome and opportunity disparities. This view gives us tools not only to understand but to address socially unjust outcome and opportunity disparities and complex and adaptive educational issues such as disproportionality. The participatory social justice perspective requires a paradigm shift: *Disability is a sociocultural construction.*

SOCIAL CONSTRUCTION OF DISABILITY

[a] blind person will remain blind and a deaf person deaf, but they will cease to be handicapped because a handicapped condition is only a social concept ... Blindness by itself does not make a child handicapped. Blindness ... is a sign of the difference between his behaviour and the behaviour of others. (Vygotsky, 1993, p. 83)

Disability is not just about people lacking/missing a general pervasive mood of happiness or sight or hearing. It is about disabling power in/of a culture in which certain differences are recognized as moral, intellectual, or medical borders. And it is about how those differences are made consequential by degrading some people and preventing them from access to certain socio-political spaces and positions and from participating in certain activities across formal and informal learning environments. McDermott and Varenne (1998) summed up that it takes a whole culture of people, their institutions, and economy and political arrangements of positioning and untiringly recording people and their actions as failures and disabilities. And the US schools are very well organized to label and disable.

The cultural infrastructural work of disability often goes unnoticed. The cultural processes such as classification of students based on ability and the tools and assumptions (e.g., extreme individualism or cultural difference as deficit) used in those processes are institutionalized and naturalized; hence became invisible. Social construction of disability does not imply that disability is not real. Rather, it means that disability is not an individual property but a matter of social structure in which the other social constructions such as race come into play to determine the educational outcomes and opportunities. Social constructivists suggest it is one kind of problem to have a behavioral range different from social expectations or use a wheelchair; it is another kind of problem to be in a culture in which others use that difference for degradation and exclusion from full participation. The latter problem is the worse (Varennne & McDermott, 1999).

My definition of participatory social justice aims at appreciating complexity of lives, experiences, and identities of non-dominant cultural groups and how individuals use and make cultures either to enable or constrain students. This definition is a seemingly simple one but it can be extremely challenging specifically for educators as it requires a critical exportation of what is conventional or normal so that we can challenge the well established ways of teaching, learning, and performing for teachers and students. Our training and practice in education, specifically in special education, has an extreme focus on finding what is wrong with a child. Instead of asking what is wrong with a student who brings underprivileged cultural, linguistic, and ability differences and struggle in schools, the question ought to be how and why certain differences are identified and made consequential in that specific school culture for that child. We should explore why and how the certain academic and social opportunities, privileges, and status are made available for some students in local schools as well as the US education system along the lines of race, language, and social class.

Participatory social justice aims to proliferate pluralism in schools not melting away of differences. As Young (1990) stated, social justice demands "institutions that promote reproduction of and respect for group differences without oppression." Democratic schools with inclusive social climates can promote social justice depending on the degree to which all stakeholders (e.g., teachers, students, families, and communities) are included in the decision-making and problem solving processes and have the opportunity to influence the outcomes (Bal, King Thorius, & Kozleski, in press). Socially just democratic schooling is not about "valuing" different cultural groups with different abilities or disabilities so that those students and their families can better adapt to conventional ways of speaking, writing, thinking, and being but challenging and transforming those monolithic and exclusionary educational practices that are designed to be perceived as natural, reasonable, wiser, and normal. Rather, it should be about using cultural, linguistic, and ability differences that non-dominant students and families bring to schools as resources to design better learning opportunities for all students, not just for minority students.

Decades of special education research show us that programmatic inclusion of students with disabilities into general education is socially and academically beneficial for both students with disabilities and students without disabilities. Moreover, two-way bilingual education programs are beneficial for bilingual students as well as monolingual English speaking students. The current global economic system highly demands a workforce that can *navigate across multiple cultural and linguistic spaces, function under uncertain ever-changing situations, and closely work with people with different backgrounds. Therefore, it is counterintuitive to force diverse students who have instrumental skills of orchestrating of multiple cultural practices, demands, and differences to assimilate into monolingual and monocultural schools that are dysfunctional to prepare the well-rounded citizens of a global world. Utilizing complex life experiences, voices, and cultural and linguistic practices that non-dominant students and families bring to schools as invaluable educational resources that are beneficial for learning and development for all students must be a core responsibility of the US schools.*

CONCLUSION

In this chapter, I argue for a critical view of participatory social justice for reframing educational inequities that non-dominant students experience in schools (e.g., disproportionality). The socially unjust outcome disparities are the tip of an iceberg. They are symptoms of larger structural processes that marginalize and exclude non-dominant students and communities at the intersections of race, class and ability. Social injustice is not a natural order but a sociocultural process reproduced through daily work and interactions of people, institutions, and ideals; hence it is open for change via concerted social action from the ground-up. My view of social justice deals with the formation of inclusive and democratic educational institutions in which diversity is valued and used for facilitating high quality learning opportunities and positive school climates for *all*.

EXTENSION QUESTIONS/ACTIVITIES

1. Individuals who look different pay a high price for their visibility in society. Bal's parents who lived in Turkey both had physical disabilities and were illiterate. Bal points to their struggles. How would they fair today in the United States?

2. Social justice is not a static state, the ultimate fairness, but a continuous collective struggle. In other words, whatever we do or do not do in our daily lives has real implications in the lives of the others who posit less power since our actions can either challenge or reproduce socially unjust processes that starts from our lives. React to these statements and then discuss with your colleagues.

3. Bal's definition of participatory social justice aims at appreciating complexity of lives, experiences, and identities of non-dominant cultural groups and how individuals use and make cultures either to enable or constrain students. Respond to Bal's definition both personally and professionally.

4. Is disability a social construction? Defend your point of view.

REFERENCES

Anyon, J. (2005). *Radical possibilities: Public policy, urban education, and a new social movement.* New York: Routledge.

Bal, A., King-Thorius, K. A., & Kozleski, E. (in press). *Culturally responsive positive behavioral support matters.* Tempe, AZ: The Equity Alliance.

Banks, J. A., & Banks, C. A. M. (2007). *Multicultural education: Issues and perspectives* (6th ed.). Boston: Allyn and Bacon.

Civil Rights Data Collection (2012). A snapshot of opportunity gap data. Retrieved March 20, 2012, from http://ocrdata.ed.gov/.

Darling-Hammond, L. (2010). *The flat world and education.* New York: Teachers College.

Losen D., & Orfield, G. (Eds.). (2002). *Racial inequity in special education.* Cambridge, MA: The Civil Rights Project, Harvard Education.

Kozol, J. (2005). *The shame of the nation.* New York: Three Rivers.

Rawls, J. (1999). *Theory of justice.* Cambridge, MA: Belknap.

Soja, E. W. (2010). *Seeking spatial justice.* Minneapolis: University of Minnesota.

Suarez-Orozco, C., Rhodes, J., & Milburn, M. (2009). Unraveling the immigrant paradox: Academic engagement and disengagement among recently arrived immigrant youth. *Youth & Society, 41*(2), 151-185.

Varenne, H., & McDermott, R. (1998). *Successful failure: The school America builds.* Boulder, CO: Westview.

Vygotsky, L. (1993). *The collected works of L. S. Vygotsky. Volume 2: The fundamentals of defectology* (R.W. Rieber & A.S. Carton, Eds.). New York: Plenum.

Young I. M. (1990). *Justice and the politics of difference.* Princeton, NJ: Princeton University.

Wortham, S. (2006). *Learning identity: The joint emergence of social identification and academic learning.* New York, NY: Cambridge University.

Aydin Bal
University of Wisconsin

GILBERT R. GUERIN AND LOUIS G. DENTI

KINDNESS IS SOCIETY: DROPPING OUT AND THE VEIL OF SOCIAL JUSTICE

The appalling school dropout rate in the United States is a seasonal issue for most Americans. Concern peaks when the news media periodically reports poor state and national dropout statistics and makes unfavorable comparisons with other industrialized nations in the world. Public interest quickly fades as other local and national concerns become news. The repercussions of the high dropout rate, where (at least) 25% of our students do not graduate (Obama, 2011), continues to seriously impact our society long after public concern abates.

This article examines the costs to individuals and to our society when students leave school before graduation. It examines ways to predict individual dropouts and to identify schools that are "dropout factories." These predictions can most often be made long before dropping out occurs. Also identified are causes for leaving school and methods for reducing the number of dropouts. In the light of known predictions and solutions, it identifies issues of social justice that result from insufficient school and societal action. It poses the question as to why injustice persists in the face of known causes and effective solutions.

IMPACT

An invisible problem

For many, perhaps for most citizens, the school dropout problem is invisible. Most adults have very little contact with the large numbers of school-aged youth who are out of school. The significant high dropout rate is barely noticed by many teachers and school personnel because dropouts often occur between semesters or at the point of grade transitions. Even within-semester dropouts are often not noticed because frequent absences mask the act of leaving school. In schools with excessively high dropout rates the behavior can become so expected that it appears to be "normal" behavior.

Dropouts are a cumulative problem with an increasing impact on a class over time. An entering 9th grade class may only lose 8% of its enrollment in the first year of high school but will continue to lose students each year until graduation at the end of grade 12. By the end of 4 years the class enrollment may have dropped by 25%. Cumulative measures provide a fairly accurate way to determine the dropouts over 4 years. If you begin to track students in the 8th grade you will find a higher number of dropouts by the end of the 12th grade.

Louis G. Denti and Patricia A. Whang (eds.), Rattling Chains: Exploring Social Justice in Education, 111–120.
© 2012 *Sense Publishers. All rights reserved.*

Workforce and the economy

The effect on our work force is one of the most obvious results of high school dropouts. Over the short term, there can be some positive impact. The pool of undereducated youth can provide workers to fill jobs that require minimum skills, especially when the demand for these workers is high. Working youth can also provide immediate money to support low-income families and can support youth who leave their families.

In the long term, the presence of a large undereducated workforce has a negative impact on the individual worker, the community, and the nation. The economic impact on the individual is easy to observe. For many, the "lack of an education" limits employment opportunities and locks individuals into work that is below their ability. Income projections for these individuals are low, job security minimal, and advancement limited. The average income for high school dropouts (ages 18 through 67) in 2009 was $23,000 versus an income of $42,000 for high school graduates, including those with General Educational Development (GED) certificate (U.S. Dept of Commerce, Census Bureau, 2009). Over a lifetime the average loss in income is $630,000 (Rouse, 2007).

One measure of the fragility of employment of the workers without a high school diploma is their employment rate, especially during periods of high unemployment. In December 2010 the rate of unemployment in the United States stood at 9.4 percent. For workers over 25 years of age the unemployment rates stood as follows: average percent of unemployment in the total workforce – 8.1; with less than a high school diploma – 15.3; those who graduated high school but without any college – 9.8; some college or associate degree – 8.1; and with a bachelor's degree and higher – 4.8. (U.S. Bureau of Labor Statistics, January 2011).

A lower standard of living for most dropouts and their families is a result of limited earnings. Low income, also, results in greater demands for assistance from social systems (i.e., Food Stamps, Temporary Aid to Needy Families). In addition, the lower income affects the community through lower purchase of commodities and services, and lower contributions in personal taxes and sales taxes. (Freudenberg, 2007).

High national productivity has become extremely important in our increasingly global economy. Nations compete in the marketplace to maintain a strong economy. This competition requires a citizenry that achieves high levels of creativity, productivity, and service. In a global market nations must compete with other nations that have larger pools of educated and creative manpower (Alliance for Excellent Education, 2007). Gordon (2009) predicts that "without drastic talent creation changes between 2010 and 2020, the United States will experience a major talent meltdown with 12 to 24 million vacant jobs across the entire U.S. economy" (p. 35). It is essential to the health of the economy to meet the challenge of preparing all the nation's youth.

Criminal justice

The data on dropouts and elevated levels of crime among this group of youth should come as no surprise. Youth who are out of school have far more free time in which to engage in mischievous and criminal behavior. "Idle time is the devil's workshop" can describe the out-of-school behavior of some youth. Simple acts of youthful mischief that lead to even casual contact with law enforcement can easily escalate to more serious misbehavior through mishandling by the individual, the police, the justice system, or the parents. Increased association with other youth with similar problems increases the opportunity for added misbehavior and for an anti social self-perception and identity.

The ineffective or antisocial behavior that leads some youth to leave school elevates the likelihood of inappropriate behavior outside school. The inappropriate behavioral characteristics that are evident in conflicts between youth and adults in the home, the school and the community can have more serious consequences when they involve law enforcement (Chapman et al., 2010). For instance, a characteristic inability to communicate civilly and effectively with adults can lead law enforcement to act more harshly when confronted with a minor infraction involving a belligerent or inarticulate youth.

Unfortunately, criminal behavior by school dropouts does not end, as youth become adults. Jones (in Sun et al., 2009) remarked, "Dropping out of high school is an apprenticeship for prison." Overall 41% of inmates in state and federal prisons have less than a high school education. Increasing the high school graduation rates by one percent would save the U.S. as much as 1.4 billion dollars per year in criminal justice costs (Dianda, 2008).

Over nine percent (9.4%) of 16-24 year old out-of-school males in the US were institutionalized in 2006-2007 while only 4.3% of high school students or graduates were institutionalized. By contrast, only 1.7% of youth who had some college or were college educated were incarcerated. Both the length of incarceration and the rate of recidivism are higher for dropouts than for high school graduates. The financial impact of criminal behavior on our society is immense.

Health issues

The health issues associated with youth who leave school early can extend over the youths' lifetime. The lifespan of dropouts is shorter than those who complete school and by many indices they are less healthy and require more medical care throughout their life. Nicholas Freudenberg (2007) reports that "If medical researchers were to discover an elixir that could increase life expectancy, reduce the burden of illness, delay the consequences of aging, decrease risky health behavior, and shrink disparities in health, we would celebrate such a remarkable discovery. Robust epidemiological evidence suggests that education is such an elixir."

Social services

The demand for public social services is higher for school dropouts than for graduates because of health, social, behavioral, and economic conditions. The demand results from both the increased need for service, the limited ability to pay for service, and the delay in obtaining adequate services. Personal habits, environmental conditions, delay in seeking help, lack of personal support systems can lead to the increased demand for service and the reliance on public vs. privately funded institutions, e.g., private mental health providers or enrolled group health care plans (Freudenberg, 2007).

Legacy

The impact of not completing school does not end with its effects on the individual. The legacy carries on with the youth's offspring's and other family members. The negative effects of dropping out of school can be transferred to the children of dropouts through lower parental expectations, motivation, and modeling. The result can be an increased potential for the offspring's school failure. The low-income family is also likely to live in a low-income section of the city where the dropout rate is higher among school peers and where school support systems are weaker. Parents may discover that they are as ineffective in helping their children cope with school failure as they were with their own school failures. The cycle of failure can persist with the child trapped into repeating the parents' ineffective patterns.

WHO DROPS OUT? CAUSES AND CONDITIONS

The evolution from student to dropout is usually a gradual process. Both the causes and the consequences of dropping out of school are well documented and dropout behavior can be predicted with some degree of accuracy as early as the 3rd-4th grade based on failures in reading. By the 8th grade failures in English, social science, and math become highly predictive of future dropouts.

Targeted efforts to improve reading can have a significant, positive impact on future learning in all subjects that rely on reading skills (e.g., social sciences, English, math, and science). Without improved reading skills and/or accommodations that support learning in reading-dependent subjects future school failure is clearly predictable. Persistent supported learning in academic areas as well as a program of adult literacy can significantly improve student performance and high school graduation rates.

Other major causal conditions include individual student characteristics, societal influences, and school conditions. Individual characteristics and the influence of society include: poor school performance; disinterest and non-engagement in school; non-English background; economic necessity; social/behavioral problems, drugs, and illness; pregnancy and early parenting; family or individual crisis; and homelessness. Societal influences include: urban environment; negative Influences by peers and gangs; negative cultural and societal attitudes, and low income. The school conditions include: a school culture that supports "pushing out" challenging students; inappropriate, inadequate, or unresponsive curriculum; inadequate school or community support systems; disengaged faculty and/or staff; and poor communication with parents and the community (American Psychological Association, 2010). However, schools and school districts that have implemented targeted and comprehensive programs designed to increase graduation rates from 9th through 12th grade students have made consistent and significant improvements in graduation rates.

The characteristics or conditions that lead students to leave school early can occur in isolation or, most often, in combination. Schools and communities that anticipate, attend and plan can reduce and mitigate many, if not all, the characteristics or conditions that lead to dropping out of school. Few conditions occur abruptly, most are observed long before a student leaves school. Even conditions that do occur suddenly, such as pregnancy or death of a family wage earner, can be mitigated with supportive school programs and social services designed to accommodate or correct the student's immediate and extended situation. Some schools and communities take effective action to hold students in school while others do not.

Balfanz (2010) reports that when students describe the reason(s) they left school they report that they did not get along with other students and/or teachers, were failing and couldn't keep up with school work, didn't like school, didn't feel safe, needed to support a family and couldn't manage both school and work, had a drug or alcohol problem, or became pregnant, married or a parent. Balfanz (2010), further reports that in the 2008 statistics the dropout percentages by ethnicity were as follows: 9% Asian, 19% White, 36% Hispanic, 38% African American. The largest proportions were from urban and poor demographic areas. Dropout rates for youth living in families with earning in the lowest quartile are 7 times higher than youth living in families with incomes in the highest quartile (Chapman et al., 2010). Both ethnicity and urban poverty are powerful factors in the dropout equation.

PREDICTING DROPOUTS AND TAKING ACTION

High school graduation rates

The current graduation rate for a high school can be predicted with a fair degree of accuracy from its history of past graduation success. Rates can vary greatly between schools and give an indication of the school's "Promoting Power" (Balfanz & Legters, 2004). Schools with the lowest success rates, those that loose 40% or more of their students before graduation, have been characterized as "dropout factories, " or more recently the "lowest performing high schools." Those who graduate 90% or better have been characterized as "highest performing schools. Approximately 20% of all students are educated in schools at each end of the graduation/dropout spectrum (Alliance for Excellent Education, 2011). The lowest performing schools tend to be in low income, minority dominated areas, the highest performing schools in affluent, white areas. The injustice to students occurs as a result of schools' failure to act or to act in an effective manner.

Individual warning signs

The basic warning signs that an individual will not graduate from high school include poor school attendance, cutting class, poor behavior, and low grades and achievement, especially in literacy (reading), and math. For many students these signs are evident by the 6th grade (Balfanz & Legters, 2006). Any one or any combination of these signs are clear indicators of a student at-risk for school failure. In addition, there are clear disparities between race/ethnicity and between genders and their dropout rates (American Psychological Association, 2010; Chapman et al., 2010).

So, where is the mystery? We can pinpoint the students who will likely leave school. We can target and ameliorate many of the problems that cause dropouts by supporting parent, school, and community interventions. We can often use existing resources or reallocate resources to implement corrective action. What is needed is individual and collective intention and will to act creatively and decisively on what we already know.

Improving school-wide programs

We know that a school can survey its school records and determine the level of performance that, over time, predicts the school's future dropouts (tools at National High School Center, Early Warning Systems, 2011). Even more simply, a school can use the predictive performance levels identified by other similar schools in estimating the characteristics of their own high-risk students. Pinkus (2008), for instance, described a number of examples of early-warning signs identified by schools and school systems. In one example (Pinkus, 2008), the New York City Department of Education found that 93% of their dropouts were "over-age and under-credited" (p. 6). They instituted multiple pathways for students who fit this profile, including small transfer schools and evening programs. Their programs resulted in significant improvements in graduation rates.

Establishing data on the warning signs of school failure is an important starting point in improving school graduation rates. Early warning data can help schools determine a) students in need of assistance, b) type(s) of assistance that could be helpful, c) grade levels at which to introduce student assistance, d) procedures for monitoring progress, and e) necessary program adjustments. The commitment to act on the basis of early warning signs is among the first steps in taking control of the dropout problem.

Improving lowest performing schools: The dropout factories

According to Balfanz and Legters (2006) "the nations Dropout Factories need to be fixed or replaced" (p. 3). Radical school restructuring is needed to break old

116

patterns and introduce new attitudes and ideas. Significant changes often require dramatic shifts in personnel and structure. These shifts may include closing the school or reassigning teachers, and replacing administrators. Even these changes are likely to fail without increased resources, significant curriculum changes, teacher training, strong parent involvement, and community participation.

If a professional, parent, or policy maker wishes to make a difference in the graduation rate at any high school, low performing or not, they need to become informed. A wealth of information on all the aspects of high school performance and school dropouts is available on the Internet. One useful source can be found at the National High School Center http://www.betterhighschools.org/topics/DropoutStrategies.asp.

In-class programs

Data generated at the school level can help classroom teachers identify student needs and plan action to improve the effectiveness of their teaching and the holding power of their class and school. Individually or in small teacher groups they can determine changes that could improve student engagement and performance. Teaching strategies that can increase student success include "personalizing instruction, providing extra learning time, striking a balance between relevance and rigor, and providing support for students who are struggling with skills or content (Pinkus, 2008, p. 4).

Realistically, both school and teacher improvements can add an extra burden to the teaching and service staffs. In order to reduce those burdens to manageable proportions requires defining and prioritizing those students to be included, program improvements to be implemented, and appropriate staff support. Some changes will need policy decisions and others might best be accomplished with the involvement of parents, community services, and collaborative community assistance (Pinkus, 2008). A dedicated teacher and a dedicated staff can significantly improve student and school performance. The evidence abounds.

SOCIAL JUSTICE AND SELF-INTEREST

In the United States we pride ourselves on a system of free public education and compulsory education laws. There is a widespread assumption that youth enter and complete school. For far too many youth, this is an illusion; for society, it is a veil of justice that obscures the actual situation.

For many youth, effective education ends early in their school careers and culminates in withdrawal from school before graduation. Some youth leave voluntarily while others are pushed out. In both cases the intent of educational laws is thwarted, justice is not served, and the impact on the individual, the community, and the society is destructive.

On the surface it would appear that the school dropout problem is a mystery that is unpredictable and without solution. The opposite is the case. The causes, predictions, results, and solutions are well documented. Years of research have

117

demonstrated that dropout behavior can be predicted with a high degree of accuracy, that the causes of failure are well known, and that some high schools contribute disproportionately. Also, the negative consequence of the failure to complete high school for the family, community, and nation can be disastrous.

Social justice demands that the laws that assure public education for all and that require regular school attendance become a reality for all students and that education serve the needs of both individuals and society. Commonly held goals of public education include the following: to prepare children for citizenship, cultivate a skillful workforce, teach cultural literacy, help students to become critical thinkers, and prepare students for the option of college (Roundtable, Inc., 2001). To achieve these goals the educational system needs to respond to differences in its students' backgrounds, skill levels, interests, and behavior. Falling short of the opportunity and goal of high school graduation for all students is an injustice to students, their parents, and the society. We as a society deserve better and can do better. Our economic future depends on it.

EXTENSION QUESTIONS/ACTIVITIES

1. Dropout continues to be a major problem in American schools and for the greater society at large. Is this an intractable problem that we must live with, or is there a veil over "dropping out of school" that distracts from dealing with this pernicious problem.

2. Guerin and Denti indicate over and over that we know what to do but have not directed our energies and resources in a systematic manner to make a significant impact on the dropout problem. Refer back to the article and jot down key points made by the authors that substantiate their point of view about dropouts. Now, craft a few thoughts of your own regarding the dropout problem and how you think it should be dealt with. Note where you agree or disagree with the arguments posited by the authors.

3. According to Guerin and Denti, "Social justice demands that the laws that assure public education for all and that require regular school attendance become a reality for all students and that education serve the needs of both individuals and society." The authors use a very strong verb, *demands*, to make their point about social justice. Respond to the quote and to the authors intent. Share your thoughts with in a colleague or in a small cooperative group arrangement.

REFERENCES

Alliance for Excellent Education. (2007). *The high cost of high school dropouts. What the nation pays for inadequate high schools.* Issue Brief (October). Washington, DC: Author.

Alliance for Excellent Education. (2010a). *Adolescent literacy.* Issue Brief (April). Washington, DC: Author.

Alliance for Excellent Education. (2010b). *Prioritizing the nation's lowest-performing high schools.* Issue Brief (September). Washington, DC: Author.

American Psychological Association. (2010). *Facing the school dropout dilemma.* Washington, DC: Author. Retrieved January 15, 2011, from http://www.apa.org/pi/families/resources/school_dropout_prevention.aspx.

Balfanz, R. (2010). *Building a grad nation: Progress and challenge in ending the high school dropout epidemic.* Civic Enterprises Everyone Graduates Center.

Balfanz, R., & Legters, (2005). *The graduation gap.* Policy Brief, Center for the Social Organization of Schools Johns Hopkins University. Retrieved from http://web.jhu.edu/CSOS/graduation-gap/power/policy.html.

Balfanz, R., & Legters, N. (2006). *The graduation rate crisis we know and what can be done about it.* Education Week Commentary. Baltimore, MD: Center for Social Organization of Schools, Johns Hopkins University.

Brindis C., & Philliber S. (1998). Room to grow: Improving services for pregnant and parenting teenagers in school settings. *Education and Urban Society, 30,* 242-260.

Chapman, C., Laird, J., & KewalRamani (2010). *Trends in high school dropout and completion rates in the United States: 1972–2008.* NCES 2011-012, U.S. Department of Education. Footnote 3, page 1.

College Board. (2010). *Three – Implement the best research-based dropout programs.* Retrieved June 30, 2012, from http://completionagenda.collegeboard.org/recommendations/3.

Dianada, M. R. (2008). *Preventing future high school dropouts.* National Education Association. Washington, DC. Retrieved from http://www.nea.org/assets/docs/dropoutguide1108.pdf.

Feudenberg, N., & Ruglis, R. (2007). Re-framing school dropout as a public health issue. *Preventing Chronic Disease – Public Health Research, Practice, and Policy, 4*(4), 1-11.

Gordon, E. (2009). The global talent crisis. *The Futurist, 43*(4), 34-39.

Jones, E. (2006). *From an address by Jones, the Illinois State Senate President at a Chicago conference on high school dropout problems in Illinois.* The Consequences of Dropping out of High School by Sum et al. (2009).

Legters, N., Balfanz, R., & McPartland, J. (2002). *Solutions for failing high schools: Converging visions and promising models.* Baltimore, MD: Center for Social Organization of Schools, Johns Hopkins University.

National Center on Secondary Education and Transition (NCSET). (2006). *The role of parents in dropout prevention: Strategies that promote graduation and school achievement.* Parent Brief. Retrieved April 14, 2011, from http://www.ncset.org/publications/viewdesc.asp?id=3135.

National High School Center. *High school topic areas.* Retrieved April 14, 2011, from: http://www.betterhighschools.org/topics/.

Obama, B. (2011). *State of the Union Address.* Washington, DC.

Pinkus, L. (2008). *Using early-warning data to improve graduation rates: Closing cracks in the education system.* Policy Brief. Alliance for Excellent Education. Washington, DC.

Roundtable, Inc. (2001). *School the story of public education.* Retrieved June 30, 2012, from: http://www.pbs.org/kcet/publicschool/get_involved/guide_p2.html.

Rouse, C. E. (2007). Quantifying the costs of inadequate education: Consequences of the labor market. In C. R. Belfield & H. M. Levin (Eds.), *The price we pay: Economic and social consequences of inadequate education* (pp. 99-124). Washington, DC: Brookings Institution Press.

Sum, A., Khatiwada, I., McLaughlin, J., & Palma, S. (2009). *The consequences of dropping out of high school: Joblessness and jailing for high school dropouts and the high cost for tax payers.* Boston, MA: Center for Labor Market Studies, Northeastern University.

Swartz, W. (2010). *New information on youth who drop out: Why they leave and what happens to them.* Retrieved June 30, 2012, from http://www.parentsassociation.com/education/drop_outs.html.

Swartz, W. (1996). *School dropouts: New information about an old problem.* ERIC Digest.

Tylera, J., & Lofstromb, M. (2010). Is the GED an effective route to postsecondary education for school dropouts? *Economics of Education Review, 29,* 813-825.

U.S. Department of Commerce, Census Bureau. (2009). Current Population Survey (CPS).

U.S. Bureau of Labor Statistics. (2011). *The employment situation.* December 2010, New Release, USDL-11-0002.

Gilbert R. Guerin
Emeritus, San Jose State University

Louis G. Denti
California State University Monterey Bay

WAYNE SAILOR AND NIKKI WOLF

KINDNESS IS SOCIETY: CHARTER SCHOOLS, DEMOCRACY, AND SOCIAL JUSTICE

We have elected to define social justice pragmatically. More specifically, the practice of social justice in a nation reflects the values embodied in that nation's constitution. A nation's highest court interprets its laws and its government enacts its policies on the basis of the constitution. Therefore, systems established by that nation to address the needs of its citizens, such as education, welfare, defense, etc., can be examined to determine the extent to which they reflect those constitutional values. When the practices of a nation's systems authentically reflect that nation's constitutional values, social justice can be said to be in play.

The United States is a western capitalist democracy. Embodied in its constitution are elements that clearly imply a welfare state, or by "welfare state" we refer to tax supported systems for education, health, public welfare (including child welfare), etc. Emancipation (i.e., civil rights) for example, is a constant theme in the development of American public policy and Supreme Court rulings. *Brown v. Board of Education* presents a landmark example of adjustments to a welfare state system, education in this case, brought about to bring that system in greater alignment with constitutional values and in so doing, bringing about a measure of social justice.

Democracy is about individual pursuit of self-interest through elected representation at various levels of government. Democratic choices are, of course, dependent upon access to information. As such, democracy is an essentially liberal endeavor since it reflects demand side (i.e., consumer) interests.

Capitalism is about pursuit of profits. American businesses and their big brothers, the multi-national corporations, represent producers' interests and, as such, have a stake in rulings and policies that are frequently diametrically opposite to those of consumers' interests. This clash of ideals is particularly intense in America because of our two-party system. Democrats, at least since the reconstruction, have been primarily identified with consumer interests and Republicans with the producers. This polarization has become more intense in recent years with the Republican Party becoming more conservative (i.e., intensely supply side in philosophy) and producer oriented. The present debate in Congress nicely illustrates this contrast of philosophies. Republicans favor preventing tax increases for corporations and the very wealthy, and seek to raise the limit on tax exceptions for inheritance to five million dollars. Democrats favor the opposite plus extending unemployment benefits for the jobless and keeping middle class tax rates from rising.

Louis G. Denti and Patricia A. Whang (eds.), Rattling Chains: Exploring Social Justice in Education, 121–126.
© 2012 *Sense Publishers. All rights reserved.*

One constant in the ever shifting political landscape is that capitalism, to survive, requires a welfare state. That is why the recent Supreme Court decision allowing corporations to provide unlimited, undisclosed contributions to political campaigns is arguably one of the most dangerous high court decisions in the history of the republic. Increasingly, access by the many to the free flow of information is coming under the control of a few (e.g., media mogul, Rupert Murdoch). It has been estimated that as many as 20% of Americans take what they learn from Fox News as factual. A one-two punch of near absolute control of access to information by producer-oriented interests coupled with the unfettered ability to buy political power by those same interests could spell the death of democracy.

Capitalism has thrived in America because of the welfare state. Systems such as accessible heath care, social welfare and a free public education have served to buffer the sharp edges of capitalism (Dryzek, 1996). Ordinary people can tolerate relative circumstances of poverty as they watch sleek Mercedes' wind past on their way to stately gated homes in the hills, as long as they have access to work, shelter, information, food and protection for themselves and their family members. Blocking access to one or more of these basic welfare support systems on any meaningful scale can quickly destabilize an otherwise orderly society.

So what does all of this have to do with social justice and the issue of charter schools? Access to information, essential to democracy comes primarily in two forms, education and "news." Setting aside the issue of free flow of information essential to a democracy though the news media, let's consider the status of education in America.

Labaree (1997) noted, throughout U.S. history the three major goals of education have been democratic equality, social efficiency, and social mobility. Perhaps the goal most closely tied to the idea of social justice is democratic equality. If citizens are not able to read or look after their own financial affairs, they are unprepared to wield much power in society. In order to impact the political direction citizens must be able to inform themselves and act on opinions. This is the essence of democracy. The second and third major goals of education are more closely tied to capitalism. The second major goal, social efficiency is modeled after the industrialization of the early 20th century when education served to better prepare new immigrants to work more efficiently and effectively in factories. This increase in production was considered a powerful tool in the national and international market place. Third, economic self-interest suggests that the purpose of education is to strengthen one's ability to move up the economic scale as far as possible. This goal of education is most closely tied to capitalism.

A century ago John Dewey advanced the premise that the purpose of public schooling should be enlightenment, through which democracy would be advanced and preserved. Having schools be a tax-supported system available to all was intended to help ensure that all viewpoints would be represented. Capitalism, however, by its nature – pursuit of profits – seeks new markets and so its expansion beyond the typical relationship with private schools for the wealthy and religious is not surprising. What is perhaps surprising is the political engineering that has led to the transfer of public monies to the private sector, aided in some states by vouchers, through charterization. Even more surprising is the enthusiastic support and policy development provided to this movement by the Democratic Party under the Obama administration. The expansion of the charter school movement continues in 2011-2012 apace with public information being disseminated in large doses by corporate "documentary" films such as *Waiting for Superman* that are appearing in local theaters across the country. Much of this expansion is occurring in corporate for-profit entities such as Knowledge is Power Program (KIPP).

Privatization transfers the responsibility for education out of public hands where the motivation is social welfare, into private hands where financial gain is the motive. The primary motive behind the birth of the charter school movement centers on positioning schools in the market to promote innovation through competition (Lubienski, 2003). Innovation was considered a likely solution to the seemingly failing educational system in the United States. Indeed charter schools are noted in NCLB as a potential solution to failing schools (Hursh, 2007; Renzulli & Roscigno, 2005; Rhim, Ahearn, & Lange, 2007). After nearly 20 years of charter schools in the U.S., the results of research on academic outcomes from measures of student achievement do not reflect promising results (Ravitch, 2009).

In exchange for freedom from district and state bureaucracy, charters commit to high levels of academic achievement as a condition of their continued existence. Charter schools may be more likely to value Labaree's second goal of social efficiency, providing educational opportunities for students who are academically higher achieving, an intellectual "survival of the fittest." Some charters with selective admission policies based on academic achievement serve this goal well. High academic achievement of their students affects the contingencies under which charter schools exist; market survival through academic achievement (Stowe & Huerta, 2007).

The Charter School Dust-Up (Carnoy, Jacobsen, & Rothstein, 2000) is a helpful resource to utilize in learning more about academic achievement in charter schools. Carnoy and his colleagues consider the major research available and compare academic achievement of charter and traditional schools. They note based on "19 studies conducted in 11 states and the District of Columbia, that there is no evidence that, on average, charter schools out-perform regular public schools. In fact, there is evidence that the average impact of charter schools is negative" (p. 2). In 2006, Lubienski and Lubienski published results from the 2003 National Assessment of Educational Progress (NAEP); they looked at several 'types' of schools including public, charter and private. They concluded there was no difference in achievement across these schools when student demographics were taken into account:

> Our findings question the notion that the private sector necessarily produces better results in areas such as education. Our study suggests significant reasons to be suspicious of claims of general failure in public schools and raises substantial questions regarding a basic premise of the current generation of school reform. (p. 684)

Heubert (2002) noted that if charter schools are positioning themselves to be a model of public education for traditional public schools, charter schools must be able to serve all students, just as typical public schools are required to do. All publically funded schools, including charter schools, are responsible for providing an appropriate education for all students; which of course includes students with disabilities. In addition to the contingency requirement of positive academic outcomes, charter schools have also been motivated to provide education economically. Carr (2008), an education reporter from the New Orleans *Times Picayune* who covers the charter movement in that city offered the following:

> Part of the issue comes down to money. Providing strong special education services is not always financially advantageous – or even feasible – for charter schools. While a typical urban school system might have a special education administrator who oversees services for 6,000 students a typical charter school, for instance, might have 60 students who require support, but would still need an administrator who knows the technicalities of complicated special education laws. Schools individually run can't take advantage of the economies of scale present in larger school systems. (p. 1)

This statement highlights the conflict for many charters; there is actually a disincentive to educate students who may be more expensive; thus the market forces, which make sense in the business world, do not make sense in the social justice world of education (Berger, 2007; Simon, 2007; Wolf, 2009). This disincentive is particularly strong when considering students who need extra learning support. It does not make fiscal sense for charter schools to hire special education staff until there are several students in the building who need support. However, a condition of many chartering agreements is the commitment to provide appropriate services to any child accepted and enrolled, regardless of current staff (Wolf, 2009). The fiscal disincentive to support *all* students clashes head-on with the social justice role of public education in addition to the civil rights of students with identified disabilities. These conflicting forces surely leave charter schools in a difficult position between economic motivation and legal requirements. Additionally, because some charter schools do not have the capacity to offer the legally required supports for students with disabilities, private systems are created in the form of companies who will (Wolf, 2009); again, funneling public money into the private sector. These complex issues should be considered prior to the wholesale spread of charters in New Orleans, for example, and other cities.

Some in the New Orleans community suspected the reason behind chartering schools was privatization and profits (Adamo, 2007):

> At the center of the charter school movement, many here believe, is the profit motive, especially for national vendors providing construction, food services, security guards, and insurance to individual charter schools, consortiums of charters, and to the RSD. In replacing the system they despised, the advocates of limited government have created fields of profit for the private sector, while frequently delivering shoddy services and unfit products. Many of the charter schools themselves are in the hands of chartering entities with national profiles, KIPP and Mosaica among them. (p. 2)

Many Americans appear to be convinced, in the face of the national media blitz, that private must be better when it comes to education! The new charter schools have important sounding names; "Academy," "College Prep," "Science and Technology" along with energetic young teachers, many of whom are serving two-year terms for Teach for America, and an air of exclusivity.

We have argued pragmatically in this essay that social values are embedded in a nation's constitution and that a measure of social justice can be gleaned from deconstructing the praxis of a nation's human services systems referenced against those values. In America, social justice is inextricably tied to democracy. Democracy is dependent upon access to information with which to make informed decisions regarding representation at all levels of government. Compulsory education is one important source of this information.

America also embraces capitalism as its economic system. Capitalism, by its nature, seeks to expand into new markets, and the systems of the welfare state including tax supported education, offer fertile new ground in which to grow profits. Publically supported welfare state systems serve the important function of buffering the painful consequences of capitalist expansion. Corporate expansion into welfare state systems poses a direct threat to these buffering mechanisms and thus to democracy itself. The charter school movement reflects this expansion of capital markets into public education. The threat to social justice, as defined in this essay, is the threat to unbiased information.

EXTENSION QUESTIONS/ACTIVITIES

1. Sailor and Wolf make the claim that the expansion of charter schools poses a real threat to democracy. The tension between private/corporate interests in education versus public education continues to energize a robust political debate on how best to educate American students. Write down your thoughts about the charter movement and what it portends for the future of education in America. Be prepared to defend your points of view using information gleaned from the Sailor Wolf article or other compelling sources.

2. According to Sailor and Wolf, "When the practices of a nation's systems authentically reflect that nation's constitutional values, social justice can be said to be in play." Respond to this quote and the notion of "authenticity" in reflecting a nation's constitutional values and how those values underscore social justice.

3. Sailor and Wolf point out that the threat to social justice is the threat to unbiased information. Refer to their article to substantiate their claim. Once you have done so, jot down some of your thoughts to see if there is overlap with your ideas and theirs regarding social justice and unbiased information.

REFERENCES

Adamo, R. (2007, June). Squeezing public education: History and ideology gang up in New Orleans. *Dissent*,10.

Berger, J. (2007, October 17). A post-Katrina charter school in New Orleans gets a second chance. *New York Times*. Retrieved December 12, 2007, from http://www.nola.com/.

Carnoy, M., Jacobsen, R., Mishel, L., & Rothstein, R. (2000). *The charter school dust-up: Examining the evidence on enrollment and achievement.* New York: Teachers College Press.

Braun, H., Jenkins, F., & Grigg, W. (2006). *A closer look at charter schools using hierarchical linear modeling* (NCES No. 2006-460). Washington, DC: Government Printing Office.

Carr, S. (2008, January 5). Charter schools struggle to meet special education needs. *The Times-Picayune*. Retrieved April 3, 2007, from http://www.nola.com/news/index.ssf/2008/01/charter_schools_struggle_to_me.html.

Dryzek, J. S. (1996). Is more democracy possible? In *Democracy in capitalist times* (pp. 3-34). New York: Oxford University Press.

Heubert, J. P. (2002). *Schools without rules? Charter schools, federal disability law, and the paradoxes of deregulation.* Wakefield, MA: National Center on Accessing the General Curriculum. Retrieved January 15, 2008 from http://www.cast.org/publications/ncac/ncac_schools.html.

Hursh, D. (2007). Assessing No Child Left Behind and the rise of neoliberal education policies. *American Educational Research Journal, 44*, 493-518.

Labaree, D. F. (1997). *How to succeed in school without really learning: The credentials race in American education.* New Haven, CT: Yale University Press.

Lubienski, C. (2003). Innovation in education markets: Theory and evidence on the impact of competition and choice in charter schools. *American Educational Research Journal, 40*, 395-443.

Lubienski, C., & Lubienski, S. T. (2005). A new look at public and private schools: Student background and mathematics achievement. *Phi Delta Kappan, 86*(9), 696-699.

Lubienski, S. T., & Lubienski, C. (2006). School sector and academic achievement: A multilevel analysis of NAEP mathematics data. *American Educational Research Journal, 43*, 651-698.

Ravitch, D. (2010). *The death and life of the great American school system: How testing and choices are undermining education.* New York: Basic Books.

Renzulli, L. A., & Roscigno, V. J. (2005). Charter school policy, implementation, and diffusion across the United States. *Sociology of Education, 78*(4), 344-365.

Rhim, L. M., Ahearn, E., & Lange, C. (2007). Considering legal identity as a critical variable of interest in charter schools research. *Journal of School Choice, 1*(3), 115-122.

Simon, D. (2007, December 6). BESE panel backs 8 new charters number in N.O. could rise to 49. *The Times-Picayune*. Retrieved February 21, 2008, from http://www.nola.com/.

Turnbull, H. R., Stowe, M., & Huerta, N. (2007). *Free appropriate public education: The law and children with disabilities* (7th ed.). Denver, CO: Love Publishing.

Wolf, N. (2010). A case study comparison of charter and traditional schools in New Orleans Recovery School District: Selection criteria and service provision for students with disabilities. *Remedial and Special Education.* Advance online publication. doi: 10.1177/0741932510362220.

Wayne Sailor
University of Kansas

Nikki Wolf
University of Kansas

126

CPSIA information can be obtained at www.ICGtesting.com
Printed in the USA
BVOW061951040213

312390BV00002B/41/P

9 789462 091054